D0943365

ACKNOWLEDGMENTS

FOREWORD — VI

FROM THE AUTHOR — VIII

PART 1: MODEL-BASED ENGINEERING AND AADL — 1

WHAT IS MODEL-BASED ENGINEERING (MBE)? — 1

WHY USE A MODEL? — 1

BENEFITS OF MODEL-BASED ENGINEERING — 3

REQUIREMENTS FOR MODEL-BASED ENGINEERING — 4

EXISTING MODEL-BASED ENGINEERING ENVIRONMENTS — 7

WHY DOES IT TAKE SO MUCH TIME FOR INDUSTRY TO USE MBE? — 9

WHAT IS A SOFTWARE ARCHITECTURE? — 11

WHY DOES THE SOFTWARE ARCHITECTURE MATTER? — 13

WHAT IS AADL? — 14

HOW DO AADL AND UML DIFFER? — 15

HOW DOES AADL COMPARE TO SYSML? — 17

WHO IS USING AADL AND WHY? — 18

OVERVIEW OF AADL TOOLS — 21

QUESTIONS — 23

PART 2: WHAT IS AADL? — 24

OVERVIEW OF THE AADL LANGUAGE — 24

COMPONENT DEFINITION — 30

COMPONENT TYPES — 31

COMPONENT IMPLEMENTATIONS — 36

COMPONENT EXTENSIONS — 41

COMPONENT ORGANIZATION — 42

AADL PROPERTY MECHANISM — 44

FLOWS — 46

FLOW SPECIFICATION — 47

FLOW IMPLEMENTATION — 50

END-TO-END FLOWS — 52

THE INSTANCE MODEL — 54

INTRODUCTION TO THE CASE STUDY — 58

PRESENTATION OF A SIMPLE SELF-DRIVING CAR   58

OVERVIEW OF THE AADL MODEL   59

INTERFACES AND DATA TYPES   65

PLATFORM ELEMENTS   68

DEPLOYMENT STRATEGIES   69

MODEL ORGANIZATION   75

QUESTIONS   76

PART 3: SYSTEM ANALYSIS WITH AADL   77

LATENCY ANALYSIS   77

WHAT IS LATENCY?   77

LATENCY MODELING WITH AADL   80

GENERATING LATENCY REPORTS USING OSATE   88

SAFETY ANALYSIS   97

INTRODUCTION TO THE ERROR MODEL ANNEX V2 (EMV2)   98

ANNOTATING THE CAR MODEL   125

SAFETY ANALYSIS TOOLS   129

QUESTIONS   148

PART 4: EXTENDING AADL   149

AVAILABLE EXTENSION MECHANISMS   149

WHICH IS THE BEST MECHANISM FOR YOU?   149

EXAMPLE OF AN AADL EXTENSION   150

AADL PROPERTIES   151

BENEFITS OF PROPERTIES   152

DEFINING A NEW PROPERTY   155

USING A NEW PROPERTY   158

EXAMINING PROPERTY VALUES IN A MODEL   160

USING THE PROPERTY EDITOR IN OSATE   162

LOOKING AT EXISTING PROPERTY DEFINITIONS   163

AADL ANNEXES   165

BENEFITS OF THE ANNEX EXTENSION MECHANISM   166

HOW TO IMPLEMENT AN ANNEX   167

ANNEX EXAMPLES   168

DESIGNING AN OSATE PLUG-IN   168

ABOUT OSATE INTERNALS   169

SET UP YOUR DEVELOPMENT ENVIRONMENT   170

SET UP AN INITIAL ECLIPSE PLUG-IN   171

STARTING THE HELLO, WORLD EXAMPLE   173

DISSECTING THE HELLO, WORLD PLUG-IN   177

ADAPTING THE PLUG-IN FOR AADL ANALYSIS   180

PROCESSING AADL ELEMENTS: A SIMPLE STATISTIC APPROACH   188

SECOND PLUG-IN: GENERATING MODEL REVIEW REPORTS   192

PLUG-IN DEVELOPMENT TIPS   202

QUESTIONS   211

CONCLUSION   212

ANNEXES   214

BIBLIOGRAPHY   214

TOOLS   217

ACRONYMS   218

IMPORTING THE CASE STUDY INTO OUR OSATE WORKSPACE   220

ANSWERS TO QUESTIONS   230

ABOUT THE AUTHOR   241

Acknowledgments

Because this book is a condensed extract of several years of work in the AADL community, there are many people who helped me in that process and deserve to be named! First of all, many thanks to the people who helped me directly by reviewing the book: Jérôme Hugues, Charles Holland, Christopher Cargal, Bernard Dion, and Eric Ferron. Many thanks to my technical writer, Pennie Walters, for taking the challenge of fixing my *French-glish* and turning what seemed to be a draft into something acceptable. I would also like to thank Laurent Pautet, my PhD advisor, for suggesting that I use AADL during my PhD—without him, I would have never looked at the technology (and this book would not exist). A special thanks goes to Bruce Lewis, the chairman of the AADL committee, who invited me early on to the standardization committee, where I started to make my first contributions. Thanks to all the people who supported me at the European Space Agency, especially Maxime Perrotin and Jean-Loup Terraillon, lead of the TASTE project. Many thanks to all the people who supported my work at the Carnegie Mellon University Software Engineering Institute, especially Peter Feiler (technical lead of the AADL committee), James Ivers, and James Over. Many thanks to Linda Northrop, a true leader in the software engineering research community who has been a great inspiration to me.

Finally, many thanks to Alejandra, the person who supports me on a daily basis. Without her pushing me to finish this book, I wouldn't have done it.

Foreword

As part of the AADL community for the last 10 years, I have witnessed and accompanied its adoption in various projects for the space, aeronautics, and medical domains. Other teams did the same across countries and institutions. The main driving force of AADL is its capability to capture various aspects of embedded systems, whether distributed, critical, real-time, or all in one concise notation. Yet, one missing piece was a book to help transition this technology to newcomers, both students and engineers.

Julien Delange is a long-term user and developer of both AADL and its supporting tools. With this book, he is culminating a long-running set of contributions around AADL, including some to the TASTE and OSATE toolsets, that cover modeling patterns for safety-critical systems, code generation, and analysis of plug-ins for safety and security.

Turning a significant portion of these past experiences into a book that is pleasant to read is a challenge of its own and one that is well executed in this manuscript. It aims at providing to the engineer and student communities one concise book that introduces some core aspects of AADL. Through one case study, readers will learn how to model a system and then analyze it. More importantly, they will be able to apply AADL directly thanks to the companion project that can be downloaded separately.

With this book, readers will be well-equipped to apply model-based architectural techniques to their own projects.

Jérôme Hugues

Note from the author: *Jérôme Hugues is an associate professor at the Institute for Space and Aeronautics Engineering in Toulouse, France. Jérôme is the lead developer of the Ocarina AADL toolsuite and has been an active member of the AADL standardization committee for more than 10 years.*

From the Author

I have been working on the Architecture Analysis and Design Language (AADL) for years and always felt there was a lack of resources for learning the concepts and starting to use the technology. I observed people basically being stuck, unable to apply the benefits of Model-Based Engineering (MBE) to their own projects. You can argue there are research papers on the topic, but they focus on theory and don't help people actually use MBE. I wanted to create a resource to help engineers, students, and teachers who are willing to learn how to use AADL for their own projects.

This book is a practical guide that introduces the main concepts of the language and explains how to use existing analysis features and design customized AADL tools. However, this book is not a comprehensive guide to learning AADL, mastering and using OSATE (which is probably the implementation reference for AADL), or discussing potential research projects. Much of that information is provided in the complete AADL standard and other publicly available resources. While this book covers some aspects of OSATE usage, it is not meant to be a complete and exhaustive reference: For that, please go to the OSATE website.[1]

This book follows a logical flow:
- Part 1 defines Model-Based Engineering and software architecture, and gives a high-level overview of AADL.
- Part 2 covers the main concepts of the AADL language so you understand how analysis tools work. (If you are

---

[1]   http://osate.org/

FROM THE AUTHOR

already familiar with the language, you can skip this section.)

- Part 3 explains how to use existing analysis tools to check different system characteristics, such as latency, safety, and security.
- Part 4 covers how to extend the language and design your own analysis plug-in in the OSATE modeling platform.

Throughout the book, I use a common case study to illustrate how to use the AADL language. As AADL evolves and the standardization committee refines it, the examples I use here might not remain up-to-date with the latest version of the language.

FROM THE AUTHOR

Important (Release) notes

- I keep an up-to-date version of the case study and all examples on the following GitHub repository.[2]
- The actual version of our model runs successfully with **OSATE 2.2.1.vupdate03**.[3]
- This book is **based on AADL v2.2.** It **does not** cover AADL v1 or v3.
- Graphical models are very hard to read. I include them in this book not to show their details but rather to show how they look in general and to encourage readers to generate and inspect them using OSATE.

---

[2] https://github.com/juli1/aadl-book
[3] http:/www.osate.org

Part 1: Model-Based Engineering and AADL

What Is Model-Based Engineering (MBE)?

Why Use a Model?

Your machine understands its own language (called the machine language). But only a few people who are very familiar with the low-level details of the machine can really understand it without help. Just like when you try to communicate with a person from another country whose language you don't know, there is a clear language gap between the programming language and the machine language. To make communication happen, we must bridge that gap using various techniques.

Over the years, engineers designed new languages that abstract the machine language and make it easier for humans to understand and use. Most of the time, the more you abstract the language, the easier it is to understand, analyze, and design programs without mistakes. Except for a few masochists, few people would argue that programming in C is easier than assembly. The higher abstractions help to focus on what is really important: The programmer designs algorithms using abstractions and doesn't worry about the low-level details. The compiler does the translation for him.

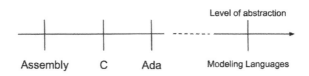

Abstraction levels: where programming and modeling languages stand

In fact, a model is nothing more than a higher abstraction level of your program, and Model-Based Engineering (MBE) simply means using models to support engineering activities (analysis, verification, implementation). Like C with assembly, a model enables you to abstract your system representation and focus on what is important. However, if computer languages aim at producing executable code, models can have different objectives, such as documenting the design or simulating the system. Of course, some modeling languages (such as the Architecture and Analysis Design Language[4] [AADL]) can also be compiled into code and ultimately transformed into binary programs, but that is not the objective of all models or modeling languages.

Using models helps you focus on what really matters in your design process. An appropriate modeling language gives you the necessary syntax and semantics to correctly describe and design key aspects of your system (concurrency, code organization, modularity, scheduling, etc.). The level of abstraction as well as the language semantics are key factors of how much analysis can be done with your language.

---

[4]   http://www.aadl.info/

Benefits of Model-Based Engineering

Models are intended to abstract your system and be used early in your design process to analyze the correctness of your system. By using models and analysis tools, you discover issues you would have discovered later, likely during your integration process. In fact, studies have shown that 70% of errors are introduced early in the design process[5] (mostly in the requirements and design phases) but are detected late, mostly during integration efforts. And they ultimately cost a significant amount of money and effort (fixing a bug in later development stages takes up to six times longer than in design stages) [NIST02, SAVI-ROI]. This inefficient process requires programmers to come back to the early phases of development, fix the design/code, and try again to integrate the system. As systems are becoming extremely software-reliant, traditional design methods are becoming time-consuming and thus, very costly.

By using models, you can detect these errors early and avoids production delays and cost increases. Of course, MBE is not a magic bullet, and the related benefits depend on your engineering domain, the methods you're using, and how well you're using them. For example, if you're developing a safety-critical system, where software analysis and validation are major concerns and many of your components were developed by independent suppliers, using MBE might detect many mistakes and help you avoid a lot of unnecessary work. But if you're using the wrong modeling language or tool, you might not catch all the errors and thus, not reap all the

---

[5]

https://www.nist.gov/sites/default/files/documents/director/planning/report02-3.pdf

potential benefits. After all, this is like any other language or tool: Selecting the wrong tool or language creates more problems than anything else. (Remember when you tried to cut a chicken using a bread knife? Probably not the best tool to use!) After all, you don't use assembly language to design a web application. The same principle applies to MBE technologies.

Requirements for Model-Based Engineering

What are the requirements for a good MBE environment? What are the criterion for a successful adoption of MBE? There is no definitive answer because it depends on your domain of expertise (web application, critical systems, etc.) and objectives (generate code, facilitate review, and create documentation).

Here's what you should look for:
- **rich and precise semantics:** The modeling language must have a precise, unambiguous semantics—an important requirement for avoiding any misunderstandings and interpretation issues between users and model-processing programs. This is a major problem with the Unified Modeling Language[6] (UML) when the same object can be represented in different diagrams (e.g., sequence and class) with different, conflicting attribute declarations (method attributes). This ambiguity raises issues: Which diagram is the correct one to use? Having a precise, unambiguous semantics upfront solves this issue. Otherwise, you just

---

[6]   http://www.omg.org/spec/UML/

introduce more problems than you solve! Unfortunately, many modeling languages fall short in this area.

- **graphical notation:** There must be a convenient and easy way to represent the model. As models are often used for documentation purposes, it is very useful to provide a graphical representation that is easy to understand (most of the time) and can be reused in the software documentation. Many modeling languages provide such a notation (e.g., UML, AADL, SCADE, Simulink).

- **user-friendly tool:** As probably one of the most important requirements, a good tool makes a big difference for the user experience and can radically change the way you see MBE. When selecting a program, make sure that it provides the necessary model-processing functions (analysis, code generation, etc.) and is easy to use. Try different tools, search online for feedback, and form your own opinion before you commit to a tool. Do not hesitate to take a few days to do your research because once you select the tool, you will use it for months or years: A mistake will significantly transform a potential success into a miserable failure. So, take your time to select a good tool.

- **open and interoperable formats:** These formats are important for three reasons:
  1. If you want to switch tools, you will be able to reuse your models and avoid a long and tedious conversion period to transition your models from tool X to tool Y.
  2. If you're communicating models with collaborators and/or people outside of your company, there is a fair chance that they use another tool. And without an interoperable format, you'll be stuck because you

won't be able to import their models (and/or they won't be able to import yours).

3. If the tool vendor goes out of business or discontinues the product, you'll need to use a different tool that can import your model.

UML uses a common representation (XML Metadata Interchange [7] [XMI]) that's used differently by each tool, blocking model reuse across modeling tools. Unfortunately, this is a way to lock people into one ecosystem. Other modeling languages (such as Matlab) use a proprietary format that changes at each version of the tool and greatly reduces competition and use of the models. The nice thing about AADL is that it addresses this issue by using a textual language that is compatible across tools so your models can be reused across tools natively.

---

[7]   https://en.wikipedia.org/wiki/XML_Metadata_Interchange

Why semantics matters

Language semantics is one of the most important requirements: Without precise semantics rules, users, and programs, the structure of your model can have different meanings and undefined behavior.

Many traditional programming languages have semantics issues, causing undetectable bugs (e.g., having an assignment as a condition – always true). Having a precise semantics avoids such issues and detects them when the model is being built instead of when it is being used.

There is a popular joke that highlights what a semantics issue is. A wife tells her husband, *"Go buy milk. And if they have eggs, buy 6."* What do you think the husband bought? Six bottles of milk. The point is this: Natural language has semantics issues. Our brain makes assumptions to bridge the gaps, but a computer cannot do that.

Existing Model-Based Engineering Environments

There are already several modeling languages and tools. Many usages focus on documentation efforts (such as the use of UML), but in some domains, modeling approaches are used extensively for system design and implementation. In fact, we can distinguish two types of modeling approaches: functional and architecture. Functional modeling languages focus on the "what" (i.e., what the system is doing), while architecture languages focus on the "how" (i.e., how the system provides a service and supports its functions).

As of today, of the two types, functional languages are used more: Before defining how a service is provided, the first concern is to define what is done. The most popular modeling languages in embedded, real-time industries are SCADE and Simulink. These two languages allow designers to specify the system behavior (order of operation, data flow) graphically, simulate the system, and then generate the final implementation using code generation. SCADE is well-known in industries with heavy design constraints (such as avionics or nuclear systems) and generates code that is automatically certified at the highest certification level for avionics systems. It has been used to create most of the Airbus on-board code since the A320, including the A340, A330, A380, and A350. Since then, the same technology has been applied to different domains (railway, medical, automotive, etc.). Companies are embracing this new MBE approach because, when used appropriately, it improves quality and reduces development costs!

Architecture languages are not focused on the "what" but rather on the "how." The two main architecture languages are SysML and AADL. SysML, which is a competitor of AADL, is a UML profile that extends the language with new diagrams and language constructs. It has the cons of other UML-related technology, especially regarding tool interoperability: It is difficult (and often impossible) to reuse SysML diagrams across tools, making use of the language tool-specific. But let's not focus on issues of SysML (there are enough articles on this!) but rather discuss how AADL can help you.

Why Does It Take So Much Time for Industry to Use MBE?

When talking about Model-Based Engineering (MBE)—also called Model-Based Design[8]—it is common to hear complaints and arguments that it is useless or worthless. Engineers might say that they tried MBE methods but saw no benefit in them. Others might claim that no project is using MBE methods and the technology is restricted to academics without any industry background who only work on a few toy examples.

These forces against the adoption of MBE are normal. Adopting MBE technologies requires you to change your development process and practices, and no one likes to change something that has worked fine for years. Change raises fear, making people initially reluctant to embrace it. But the problem is that current development techniques are insufficient for delivering new systems on time, especially embedded, safety-critical ones. We must create new techniques that will meet the requirements of new systems.

Embracing MBE approaches requires training engineers, learning new tools, and changing how you develop software. These tasks take time so, instead of developing new products, the company spends money on training engineers, which takes them away from customers. Adopting MBE requires a lot of investment in both time and money. Return on investment[9] (ROI) [SAVI-ROI] studies have shown that management may not be willing to support MBE because it

---

8   https://en.wikipedia.org/wiki/Model-based_design
9   http://savi.avsi.aero/wp-content/uploads/sites/2/2015/08/SAVI-AFE58-00-001_Summary_Final_Report.pdf

doesn't pay off after the first project and is rather a long-term investment. Why invest now when you won't be here to take credits for the results? ANSYS demonstrated that using its SCADE tool to design safety-critical systems removes a lot of costly work related to certification and ultimately pays off quickly (otherwise, Airbus would not use SCADE for new planes such as the A380 or A340 as many other companies did[10]). In the long run, you save a lot of effort, but in a world where the focus is on immediate returns, your CEO or CTO might not see that.

Ultimately, MBE will be adopted for several reasons. First of all, history has shown that when producing software, new methods and languages are abstracting concepts in order to simplify the design and implementation of software. Another reason is simple: Training costs will be reduced. New engineers will be trained in school and then join companies, ready to use MBE tools, at no cost to the company. This has already happened for behavioral modeling tools, such as SCADE[11] and Simulink[12] [SCADE, SIMULINK]. The last and most obvious reason why model-based technologies will be adopted in the long run is that companies will no longer be able to keep up with the increasing production costs. At each iteration, systems are becoming more complex, so they contain more functions that interact with each other and introduce various bugs and other side effects that are eventually detected late and require a lot of rework. As competitors that adopt MBE start to show cost reductions and improvement in the development process, other

---

[10]   http://www.esterel-technologies.com/success-stories/
[11]   https://en.wikipedia.org/wiki/Esterel_Technologies
[12]   https://en.wikipedia.org/wiki/Simulink

companies will follow. Although the change will take place slowly, it will ultimately happen. If you're wondering whether to invest in MBE technologies, you might want to think about the long-term benefits and decide if you want to be one of the early adopters.

What Is a Software Architecture?

There are many definitions of software architecture and its related terms (such as quality attribute). As Randy Pausch said in his famous "last lecture" talk[13] [LAST-LECT], Wikipedia[14] is probably the most trustworthy source, so we'll use its definition[15] [WIKI-SA]:

> *"**Software architecture** refers to the fundamental structures of a software system, the discipline of creating such structures, and the documentation of these structures. These structures are needed to reason about the software system. Each structure comprises software elements, relations among them, and properties of both elements and relations, along with rationale for the introduction and configuration of each element. The architecture of a software system is a metaphor, analogous to the architecture of a building."*

This definition might not help you as such, but I find the analogy with a building architecture very helpful in explaining the concept of software architecture. In fact, as for a building, the software architecture shows you how your

---

13   http://www.cmu.edu/randyslecture/
14   http://www.wikipedia.org/
15   https://en.wikipedia.org/wiki/Software_architecture

system is organized, what elements are connected, and what materials are used to realize it. A good building architecture makes users happy: It is easier to navigate from one room to another and stay warm during winter and not too hot during summer. Similarly, a good software architecture eases system upgrades, supports your business goals, and increases customer satisfaction.

When designing a building, the architect takes the requirements from the customer and produces an architecture. This architecture defines the foundation of the building and the organization of the space: how rooms are connected, how floors are stacked, etc. The initial requirements and constraints guide you to establish the architecture: If you don't have a lot of land, you might have several floors. On the other hand, if you have a lot of land and are building a facility for senior citizens, you might prefer to put all rooms on the same floor to avoid stairs. The purpose and context of the building are also very useful: You don't use the same foundation, materials, and floorplan for a nuclear power plant (which is life-critical) and a school. Similarly, when designing a software architecture, you must make reasonable choices that fit with your context and satisfy both your objectives and your customers.

It's easy to understand quickly what is a bad building architecture. For example, if the only door of your bathroom is connected to the living room, there are obviously some design issues with your house. Similarly, if your entry door opens into the bedroom, you might think there's a privacy concern. Such issues exist in software, but it's very difficult to detect such bad design in software.

Why?

Because software architecture is still an emerging concept. The architecture of your building is formalized using plans, contracts, and paper documents from your architect, but a software architecture is captured using various methods, languages, and tools that few people really understand. In fact, it's common to have a software architecture specified with a productivity suite such as Microsoft PowerPoint or Visio. Such tools can be useful and popular in some domains, but they are inappropriate for designing a software architecture. The choice of the correct tool must be driven by your domain of expertise and your objective. For example, in the context of IT or web systems, the software architecture helps to communicate between development teams. When using real-time systems, the model can be used not only for documentation purposes but also for analysis or even implementation.

Why Does the Software Architecture Matter?

Let's continue with the building analogy: If the architect of your house messes up its architecture, in addition to having a building that's hard to live in, you might need to do a lot of work to fix structural issues. Imagine if the garage is connected only to your bedroom or if you're living in a noisy area and the designers did not think about using materials with good isolation. Fixing these issues is a painful and expensive process. Starting on the right foot with the right architecture up front ensures that you build the right system from the beginning and avoid most potential rework efforts later. And to build the right system, you must be able to design and analyze your architecture.

When designing your software architecture, you need to make reasonable and good design decisions from the beginning so your customers are satisfied first and you avoid rework and redesign later. For a web application, those decisions might involve choosing the right framework to build your application, selecting the most appropriate database system, or ensuring that you can later easily extend the number of web servers. For a real-time system, the decisions might involve depending on a real-time operating system or selecting a deterministic bus. No matter what, you must be able to analyze the architecture to make sound design decisions.

What Is AADL?

Now that we've explained the importance of software architecture, you might wonder what AADL is about and how it relates to all of this. AADL, which stands for Architecture Analysis and Design Language, is an architecture language that targets real-time, embedded systems. It focuses on system design specification using a rich, formal semantics that can be used to analyze and generate the system.

Basically, the philosophy is that the architecture model is a central development artifact that's the backbone of your development process: Once you have the model, you can analyze the system, generate the implementation, and derive tests from it. Of course, the first model is not the one that will be implemented: Through analysis, simulation, and rapid prototyping, you refine the model and eventually come up with the correct implementation.

While the first users were mostly from the avionics domain, AADL is now used extensively in many other safety-critical domains, such as automotive manufacturing, healthcare, avionics, and the military.

How Do AADL and UML Differ?

Many people ask what the differences are between AADL[16] and UML[17] [UML]. Comparing these technologies is hard because they don't have much in common and have different objectives. UML [UML] is a great technology for modeling the organizational aspects of a system (e.g., class diagrams) and its behavior (e.g., sequence diagrams), which is basically, how you divide your software into packages, how objects interact, and so on. UML does not address safety-critical and real-time properties—that has been done with the MARTE profile[18] [MARTE], which unfortunately is no longer maintained (the latest document was published in 2011) and therefore no longer considered viable.

If you want to document how you develop a particular software and show its decomposition into classes and packages, UML is probably what you need to use. It's good at documenting software, especially when developers need to communicate the organization of class or the flow of operations between objects. However, the language has some caveats that make it not amenable for the design of embedded, real-time systems:

1. **representation inconsistencies**: As UML provides several diagrams[19] for the same system, the user can represent the same thing with different attributes. Then, what is observed (and probably analyzed) is different

---

16   http://www.aadl.info/
17   http://www.uml.org/
18   http://www.omg.org/spec/MARTE/
19

      https://en.wikipedia.org/wiki/Unified_Modeling_Language#Diag
rams

from one diagram to another. If you have two things specified differently, which one should you pick? The design process needs to rely on a consistent semantics.

2. **semantics issue**: Some elements of the UML semantics are not completely defined, so they're up to the model user's interpretation. For example, one such element is the concept of execution platform and its related scheduling properties (which indicate if the system can meet its timing constraints). Designing safety-critical systems requires a precise semantics that leaves no room for misinterpretation. AADL provides a rich and precise semantics, defined in the standard, that doesn't leave anything up to interpretation.

3. **interchange format**: UML tools use different formats to store models. Each tool implements its own format (often using XMI), but in the end, they are not interoperable across different UML tools and one model designed with tool X cannot be used by tool Y. This is unfortunate because, for example, tool X can be a great tool to design your model, but tool Y can have the analysis features you need. Or, when working with teams from different companies, one team might have tool X and the other tool Y. This problem locks people into one ecosystem, which is a bad business practice (customers choose you for the quality of your tools, not because you lock them up!). AADL solves this issue by defining a clean interoperable, textual representation. The same textual model can be imported into different tools: As long as they have an AADL parser, you are good to go!

How Does AADL Compare to SysML?

SysML is a UML profile for system modeling.[20] It adds some features, such as the parametric and requirements diagram, and others that are lacking in UML[21] (especially for system engineering), but (unfortunately) it shares the same shortcomings as its ancestor. Because it comes from UML, SysML also shares the same (dis)advantages.

SysML is a good candidate for documenting an architecture and has a graphical notation as well. For a long time, AADL lacked a tool with a good graphical support. However, many AADL tools (such as [OSATE[22]] and [MASIW[23]], see the Tools section on page 217) now support a graphical AADL editor. One interesting aspect of SysML is that, considering the number of people already familiar with UML, it has an "affordable" learning curve. While AADL has a steeper learning curve, in the long run, its precise semantics provide many more benefits than SysML does (such as better analysis capability and automatic code generation).

The table below summarizes the differences between AADL and SysML.

	AADL	**SysML**
Pros	Precise semantics Interchange format Multi-Domain Analysis code generation support	Low learning curve due to UML heritage Tool support

---

20   http://www.omgsysml.org/
21   http://uml.org/
22   http://osate.org/
23   https://forge.ispras.ru/projects/masiw-oss

Cons	Learning curve	Interchange format Semantics need to be refined

Differences between AADL and SysML

Who Is Using AADL and Why?

AADL is used all over the world. Although it was initiated in the USA, European countries were first to use it, especially in large research projects. Starting in 2004, the European Space Agency (ESA) used AADL for ASSERT: a 15 M€ European project aimed at defining a new system and software development process. It was a collaborative project lead by ESA with 20 partners from 11 countries in Europe. Following the success of ASSERT, ESA started to support TASTE, an open-source toolchain for embedded software[24] development that relies on AADL to integrate all the different system components. The platform is focused on aerospace systems but can easily be used for other families of systems (medical, avionics, railways, etc.). Through the years, ESA used TASTE to design, validate, and implement safety-critical applications. ESA still supports TASTE and is advocating for its use in operational projects and the transition of traditional development processes to MBE. ESA's efforts convinced many people in the research community to try AADL, which convinced many researchers to use the technology in other contexts as well. For example, the COMPASS[25] [COMPASS] project focused on using AADL for safety analysis, which led the Error Model Annex[26] [AADL-

---

24   http://taste.tuxfamily.org/
25   http://www.compass-toolset.org/
26   https://saemobilus.sae.org/content/as5506/1

EMV2]) and the D-MILS[27] [D-MILS] project to use AADL for security analysis. These projects also strengthened the AADL community across Europe.

While Europe was making progress in the use of MBE and AADL for architecture design and analysis, researchers in Russia gained interest in the technology. In 2010, researchers from the Institute for System Programming of the Russian Academy of Sciences (ISPRAS) joined the AADL committee and started to make significant technical contributions. A few months later, they unveiled MASIW [MASIW Tool], an AADL editor that supports both textual and graphical notations. After improving their technologies over the years, ISPRAS researchers are now able to use AADL to perform safety analysis, code generation, and system simulation.

Similarly, activity in the USA has been pretty intense with many actors using AADL in their research in different domains. The University of Minnesota and Rockwell-Collins participated in many Defense Advanced Research Projects Agency (DARPA) projects [SMACCM] and developed a lot of AADL tools (e.g., [AGREE] and [RESOLUTE]). These organizations extended the technology with a constraint language and annexes to check model properties and system behavior. The University of Pennsylvania and Kansas State University did a lot of work using AADL to design and analyze medical devices. Lastly, the Carnegie Mellon Software Engineering Institute[28] (CMU-SEI) has been a leader in the AADL technology, with Peter Feiler, an SEI fellow, as the technical leader for the standard. The CMU-SEI has

---

[27]   http://www.d-mils.org/
[28]   http://sei.cmu.edu/

applied the technology to several projects, including SAVI [SAVI], a project that regroups major avionics and aerospace companies and demonstrated the value of MBE for safety-critical software. The CMU-SEI also applied the AADL technology to multiple US Army projects to design new systems and support upgrade efforts.

The following map shows the locations of known companies, universities, and research centers using AADL. Obviously, there are still a lot of unknown organizations using the technology and some that won't admit to using it (mostly for intellectual property reasons). At the very least, the map shows a high engagement rate in the United States and Europe.

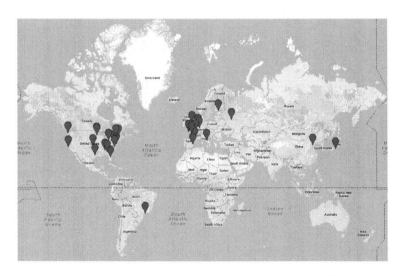

Map of companies and institutes using AADL

Overview of AADL Tools

Over the language's lifetime, universities and software companies have developed many AADL tools, which I describe below. Please be aware that having worked on Ocarina[29] and OSATE,[30] my opinion about some of them might be biased.

The most popular tool for using AADL is OSATE, which was developed by the CMU-SEI. This tool supports the latest version of the language and is mostly stable, although it has some usability and stability issues that are probably due to it being a research project. OSATE includes a textual and graphical editor as well as varied analysis tools (e.g., for latency, weight, and safety). It does not support code generation but rather includes a bridge to Ocarina to generate code. OSATE supports the core language, the Behavior Annex, and the Error Model Annex.

Ocarina is a command-line interface (CLI) tool that focuses mostly on code generation. It generates code from AADL models to various platforms such as Linux (POSIX[31]), VxWorks,[32] and DeOS,[33] and supports the textual language and the Behavior Annex.

SCADE Architect[34] is a commercial modeling platform for AADL. It doesn't use the AADL language directly but has the ability to import/export a system description from/to an

---

29   http://www.openaadl.org/
30   http://www.osate.org/
31   https://en.wikipedia.org/wiki/POSIX_Threads
32   https://en.wikipedia.org/wiki/VxWorks
33   https://en.wikipedia.org/wiki/DDC-I
34   http://www.esterel-technologies.com/products/scade-system/

AADL model. The tool lives in the Eclipse ecosystem and interfaces with all analysis functionalities from OSATE. Its main advantage is its popularity: SCADE Architect can interface AADL models with many other models (e.g., SysML) and with SCADE Suite, a great design tool for implementing system behavior.

AADL inspector,[35] from Ellidiss[36] technologies, is a tool that supports the core AADL language and its Behavior Annex. This tool, which provides the ability to simulate the system execution from a model, does not support graphical models and uses an in-house technology (Logic Model Processing) to interface with different notations and query the modeling artifacts.

MASIW,[37] from ISPRAS in Russia, is an Eclipse-based tool that supports textual and graphical modeling. It provides several analyses, including system simulation and safety analysis, and a code generator for avionics operating systems.

The table below summarizes the qualities of these AADL tools.

Tool	Languages Artifacts	Functions	License
OSATE	Core language Error Model Annex Behavior Annex	Latency analysis Safety analysis Constraints checker Graphical modeler	EPL

---

35 http://www.ellidiss.com/products/aadl-inspector/
36 http://www.ellidiss.com/
37 https://forge.ispras.ru/projects/masiw-oss

Tool	Languages Artifacts	Functions	License
Ocarina	Core language Behavior Annex	Code generation Constraint checker	GPL
SCADE Architect	Core language	Interface with SysML and other system descriptions Graphical modeler	Proprietary
AADL inspector	Core language Behavior Annex Error Model Annex	Simulation Schedulability analysis	Proprietary

Tool	Languages Artifacts	Functions	License
MASIW	Core language Error Model Annex	Safety analysis Simulation Code generation Graphical modeler	GPL

Summary of AADL tools

Questions

1. What are the main advantages of MBE?
2. What is AADL? UML? SysML?
3. Where are most errors introduced in traditional development processes?
4. Where are most errors addressed in traditional development processes?

Part 2: What Is AADL?

The Architecture Analysis and Design Language (AADL) is an architecture modeling language that captures the hardware and software aspects of a system and their interaction. The language is primarily targeted at safety-critical, real-time systems where sensors and actuators are tightly coupled with software components and facilitate analysis of interaction between hardware and software components. In this part, I provide an overview of the language and explain the case study used throughout the book.

Overview of the AADL Language

AADL is component-centric. An AADL model contains component types and implementation with their interfaces, subcomponents, and other properties. It defines the system in a hierarchical manner where the top component is called the root system.

AADL defines different types of component categories, each with a clear and precise semantics: Instead of being a box without meaning, assigning a category to a component implies that it has a particular purpose and behavior within the system. Component categories are grouped into three clusters: **hardware**, **software**, and **hybrid**:

1. **Hardware components** have a physical property, something you can physically touch or see:
   a. The `device` category represents a device, like an alarm or a sensor.
   b. The `processor` category represents a processing unit that executes code. Depending on the degree of

24

modeling and the objective of your model, you can stay at a high level of modeling or refine the implementation with more details (e.g., represent each core, cache, and internal bus of the processor).

c. The `bus` category represents a physical connection between entities (e.g., processor, system, devices). For example, it can be the Ethernet bus that connects servers in a data center or the AFDX network inside a plane.

d. The `memory` category characterizes a hardware memory on a chip or your motherboard. For example, this category might include the RAM of your desktop, a USB stick, or the micro-SD card of your camera.

e. The `virtual bus` category represents a protocol used for logical connections between software components. An AADL `virtual bus` can represent a TCP/IP protocol implementation or the SSL layer used during an HTTP connection. It's possible to encapsulate `virtual bus` components to model a protocol stack (e.g., a layer composed of an HTTP protocol on top of an SSL protocol, which is itself on top of a TCP protocol). A logical AADL port connection (between process threads) can be bound to a virtual bus to show the protocol used to transport the data.

f. The virtual processor component category is a software representation of a hardware concept. For example, a virtual machine running on a processor or an isolated partition of the execution runtime, as used in some safety-critical operating systems (such as ARINC653). The virtual processor is associated with an AADL processor component to show which underlying hardware is executing it.

2. **Software components** represent non-physical artifacts:

a. The `data` category captures a data type with its characteristics, such as the size, representation clause, or encoding. An AADL `data` component can be used in different manners: When associated with a component interface, it represents the data type used on that interface. When associated with a data subcomponent, it represents the data type associated with a shared memory (such as a global variable).

b. The `subprogram` category specifies a block of executable code with its interface (called parameters). It's a way to represent a C function, an Ada subprogram/function that's eventually executed by a thread. An AADL subprogram component can also declare its implementation language (e.g., Ada, C), its name, source file, etc.

c. The `thread` category represents an entity that executes an instruction flow (the instruction flow itself is specified with AADL subprograms). A thread is characterized by its timing constraints (e.g., period, deadline) and how it's executed (time- or event-triggered).

d. The `process` category is the representation of an address space that contains data and thread subcomponents containing the necessary elements to execute the software. It's very similar to the concept of a UNIX process.[38] The process is associated to a `processor` (that executes its thread and provides basic execution services) and a `memory` (that physically stores the memory). By itself, a `process` is simply an empty address space whose boundaries are enforced by the underlying runtime. A typical implementation of an AADL process contains AADL `data` components and AADL `thread` components that execute subprogram components.

3. **Hybrid components** do not represent anything concrete but rather are convenient constructs for specifying a component whose category can be defined later (i.e., `abstract`) or to wrap an assembly of component (i.e., `system`):

   a. The `abstract` category is used to represent components whose category is still unspecified. Such a category is useful in the early stage of system design, when requirements are still in the works and no implementation choice has been made. The designers can specify the external interfaces and component characteristics (such as timing) and later decide the appropriate component category. For example, when implementing a sensor-processing module, the designer can specify it early on as an abstract device with its interfaces (incoming and outgoing data) and later, refine it as a device (hardware implementation) or a process (software implementation). However, regardless of the selected

---

[38]
    https://en.wikibooks.org/wiki/A_Quick_Introduction_to_Unix/Files_and_Processes

category, the initial specifications (interfaces and properties) will still hold.

b. The `system` category is used to assemble components. The `system` category is a container that regroups and configures the components required to implement the system. AADL `system` components can also be used to organize the implementation in a hierarchical manner with subsystems. For example, an avionics system has different independent subsystems (e.g., sensors, flight management, logging).

The next sections of this chapter explain how to define AADL components using the textual notation and integrate them into a model. This introduction provides the knowledge you need to understand the main construct of the AADL language and start your own model. This is not a complete presentation of the language since these topics are not covered: modes, component refinement, component behavior, subprogram group, and thread group. For a complete definition of the language, you can read the full AADL standard[39] [AADL-STD], which is very long (and boring). I recommend reading it only when you need to know the exact definition of an element (in all honesty, I haven't read the whole thing).

The language is constantly evolving, and the standardization committee is currently working on the third version of AADL (AADL v3.0). While the foundations and core concepts of the language are solid, the language evolved to address issues users are facing. For that reason, the examples used here might not work with the latest version of OSATE at the time

---

[39]   http://standards.sae.org/as5506b/

of you read this book. However, we maintain examples that are up-to-date with the latest version of the language on our online code repository.[40] So even if the language evolves, you can still experiment and use the technology!

Textual or graphical notations

AADL supports two notations: **textual** and **graphical**. In the sections below, we will explain only the textual notation for the following reasons:

1. The textual version is totally standardized without ambiguity. In the graphical version, there is no standard way to represent a property (and honestly, it might be quite difficult to represent all the AADL properties graphically).

2. The textual version is ultimately what tools will read and process. It is also the common representation that's interoperable across tools. If you're using several AADL tools, you'll likely have to at least understand the textual version.

3. Graphical layers can be inefficient when navigating into a model, and the layout is often bad. A textual model avoids these issues.

4. With the textual version, you don't need any fancy editors. You can even write models using good text editors such as Vim or Emacs[41] [AADL-MOD].

---

40   https://github.com/juli1/aadl-book

41   http://www.openaadl.org/aadl-mode.html

Component Definition

An AADL model is composed of component types and implementations:

- The **component type** is the envelope of the component. It defines the component category and its external interfaces and shows how it communicates with the rest of the world. We can see it as the specification of the component (what the component is supposed to provide to the rest of the world).
- The **component implementation** defines the inside of the component: how the interfaces are connected to subcomponents to provide the service.

A component type can have multiple implementations. After all, the same services (component type) can be implemented in different ways (component implementation). This is a great approach when designing an architecture: The component type defines how the component is used and the final implementation can be chosen when integrating the components together. Also, when contracting the implementation, it is possible to provide the component type and let the contractor develop the implementation. Then, when doing the final architecture, you can just pick the architecture you really want.

To illustrate the concepts of components definition, we use a simple system that follows a usual design pattern in safety-critical systems: a sender (producer) function, a processing function, and a receiver (or actuator) function. The graphical representation of the AADL model is shown below; the textual version is provided in the sections below.

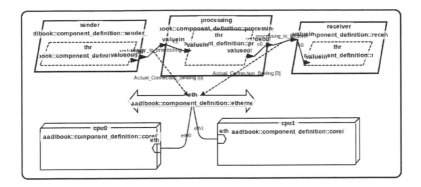

**Graphical representation of the AADL model presented
in this section**

Component Types

An AADL component type is characterized by:

- a **component category** (required): device, system, processor, process, etc.
- a **unique identifier** to identify the component
- **features** (optional) that define the component interfaces available to the outside world
- **flows** (optional) that specify how data flows from input to output ports. Flows are specified in the component type by showing how data flows in the external interfaces (features). Flows are later refined in the component implementation and described later in this section.
- **properties** (optional) that define specific characteristics of the component and/or its parts. Property usage is explained later in this section.

- **AADL annexes** (optional) that augment the component description with other languages. Examples of existing AADL annexes and how to define your own annex are detailed in Part 4 of this book.

The AADL interfaces show what the component exposes to the outside world, either physically (hardware/hybrid component) or logically (software/hybrid components). Features are classified under two categories: **ports** and **components access**:

- **Ports** represent the interaction point for an event (i.e., notification), a data transfer, or a combination of both. Ports can be specified for the following components: device, thread, process, and system. There are three types of ports:
  - The `event port` represents the emission/reception of a notification and carries a signal without any data. For example, such an event can be a health-monitoring exception or the detection of data from a sensor (e.g., temperature below a predefined threshold). When using such a port, a usual pattern is to have the software waiting on an incoming event.
  - The `data port` (exchange of data) represents an interface that receives a data flow and always keeps the latest values. The port value is updated as soon as a new data instance is received. Such a port is often used with safety-critical applications because the receiver does not have to wait for a new data instance and is sure to get a value when the software is executed.
  - The `event data port` (exchange of data with notification) combines the event port and the data

port in the same entity. The `event data port` transports a signal (`event`) associated with `data`.

Ports are characterized by a direction: `in`, `out`, or `in out`. A port is graphically represented with arrows: Depending on the type (`event`, `data`, or `event data`), the arrow is filled or empty.

- **Components access** specifies if a component `requires` or `provides` access to a particular service. For example, a processor requires access to an Ethernet bus, or a system can provide access to a bus. There are two types of access: `bus access` and `data access`, and two types of direction: `requires` component access (incoming—the component imports the component's capability) and `provides` component access (outgoing—the component exports the component's capability). The graphical representation is a big arrow filled in with white.

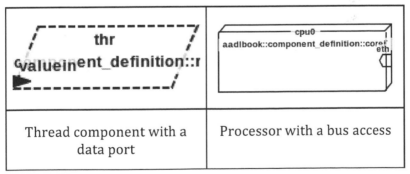

Thread component with a data port	Processor with a bus access

Graphical representation of features

The features used in our examples are shown in the figure above. On the left, there is a thread component (parallelogram with dashed line) with an incoming data port named `valuein`. On the right, there is a processor component (3D box with a line) with a component access showing that access to a bus is required (bus access named eth).

Now, let's see how to declare component types using the AADL textual notation. The following listing contains all components types of the model presented before. For example, the thread with the name receiver_thr has:

- an **incoming data port** named valuein that's associated with the data component mydata, which captures the specific requirements of the data (size, etc.)
- **two properties** to specify its dispatch_protocol (periodic) and its period (10ms). This means that the thread will be executed periodically, every 10 milliseconds.

Notice that the processing_pr component (that has the process category) has two features (data ports): valuein and valueout. Both are associated with the same data type (mydata), which has a size of 1 byte (see the Data_Size property for the mydata component).

```
thread receiver_thr
features
    valuein : in data port mydata;
properties
    dispatch_protocol => periodic;
    period => 10 ms;
end receiver_thr;

process receiver_pr
features
    valuein : in data port mydata;
end receiver_pr;
thread sender_thr
features
    valueout : out data port mydata;
properties
    Dispatch_Protocol => periodic;
    period => 20 ms;
end sender_thr;

process sender_pr
features
    valueout : out data port mydata;
end sender_pr;
thread processing_thr
features
    valuein  : in data port mydata;
    valueout : out data port mydata;
properties
    Dispatch_Protocol => periodic;
    period => 20 ms;
end processing_thr;

process processing_pr
features
    valuein  : in data port mydata;
    valueout : out data port mydata;
end processing_pr;
```

```
bus ethernet
end ethernet;

data mydata
properties
    Data_Size => 1 bytes;
end mydata;

processor corei7
features
    eth : requires bus access ethernet;
end corei7;

system integration
end integration;
```

Component types of the system

Component Implementations

A component implementation implements an AADL component type that can have multiple implementations. The name of a component's implementation is prefixed by the component types it implements, followed by a dot and the name of the implementation. For example, the component implementation name `mycomponent.impl1` is an implementation named `impl1` for the component type `mycomponent`. You can define as many implementations as you want for a type—for example, `mycomponent.impl2`, `mycomponent.impl3`, and `mycomponent.impl3`—and all of them will inherit the interfaces and properties for the component type `mycomponent`.

PART 2: WHAT IS AADL?

An AADL component implementation is defined by:

- a **component category** that specifies which category is implemented. It's the same thing as the component type being implemented.
- a **unique identifier** to use and reference the component implementation. As mentioned before, the name is prefixed by the implemented component type, followed by a dot and a unique identifier. For a component type foobar, you could have two implementations: foobar.impl1 and foobar.impl2.
- **subcomponents** (optional) that define the content of your component: what is contained in your implementation to provide the requested services. For example, a system can contain a processor and several process components bound to it. AADL legality rules define which component types can be contained in an implementation. For example, a process component can have thread and/or data but cannot contain device. These rules are just here to avoid assemblies that do not make any sense at all, e.g., a process inside data.
- **connections** (optional) that define how the component features (defined in the type) are connected to the subcomponent features. In fact, the connections are there to show how interfaces from the outside world interact with the interfaces located within the component. A connection connects one feature from the component (port or component access) to one feature from a subcomponent. For example, it is possible to connect one data port from a process to a thread or to connect a provide bus access from a system to a requires bus access from a device.

- **flows** (optional) that explain how the flow specification (from the component type) is implemented using the subcomponents. It explains how the data flows through the different subcomponents.
- **properties** (optional) that define characteristics of the component. Properties can already be defined in the component type. When a property is defined in the component implementation, this is an additional property. If the property defined in the component implementation already exists in the component type, it simply overrides the value from the component type. Property usage is explained later in this section. Part 4 of this book details how to declare your own property set or locate existing properties.
- an **AADL annex** that augments the description of the core language with another language. Annex languages are detailed in Part 4 of this book.

As for the component type, let's review how to declare the component implementation through the practical example shown below. In it, only process and system components have a declared implementation. Now, let's look at the process implementation `processing_pr.i`. First, as indicated by the name, it means that this component is implementing the component type `processing_pr` specified in the previous section. The name has the suffix `.i` to uniquely distinguish the implementation. Inside the implementation, the component defines:

- the subcomponents it contains using the subcomponent section. It actually contains one subcomponent `thr`, which has the type `processing_thr`.
- the connections with the component's interfaces and/or its subcomponents in the connection section. The implementation `processing_pr` connects the feature

`valueout` from its thread to its own output port and its own input port `valuein` to the interface `valuein` in the component `thr`.

Let's also review a system implementation that integrates all components and builds a complete system. The system integrates all the `process` components to send, `process`, and use the data. Each `process` is executed on a different `processor` component connected through a `bus` component. In order to communicate, the `process` components, distributed across `processor` components, are connected using `data port` connections that are bound to `bus` components. The component implementation `integration.i` integrates all the necessary components:

- It contains all the components required to realize the system (section subcomponents): cpu0, cpu1, cpu2, `sender`, `receiver`, `processing`, and `eth`.
- It connects the `features` from the subcomponents (section `connections`): data ports between the sender/processing/receiver process component and bus access between the cpu0, cpu1, and cpu2 processor components.
- It defines how connections are mapped to the bus using the `actual_connection_binding` property (section `properties`, explained below).
- It associates each process to a processor using the `actual_processor_binding` property.

```
process implementation processing_pr.i
subcomponents
    thr : thread processing_thr;
connections
    c0 : port thr.valueout -> valueout;
```

```
    c1 : port valuein -> thr.valuein;
end processing_pr.i;


process implementation sender_pr.i
subcomponents
    thr : thread sender_thr;
connections
    c0 : port thr.valueout->valueout;
end sender_pr.i;

process implementation receiver_pr.i
subcomponents
    thr : thread receiver_thr;
connections
     c0 : port valuein -> thr.valuein;
end receiver_pr.i;

system implementation integration.i
subcomponents
    cpu0        : processor corei7;
    cpu1        : processor corei7;
    cpu2        : processor corei7;
    sender   : process sender_pr.i;
    processing : process processing_pr.i;
    receiver   : process receiver_pr.i;
    eth        : bus ethernet;
connections
    eth0       : bus access eth <-> cpu0.eth;
    eth1       : bus access eth <-> cpu1.eth;
    eth2       : bus access eth <-> cpu2.eth;
    sender_to_processing   : port
          sender.valueout -> processing.valuein;

    processing_to_receiver : port
        processing.valueout -> receiver.valuein;
properties
    Actual_Connection_Binding => (reference
(eth)) applies to
sender_to_processing,processing_to_receiver;
    Actual_Processing_Binding => (reference
```

```
(cpu0)) applies to sender;
    Actual_Processing_Binding => (reference
(cpu1)) applies to processing;
    Actual_Processing_Binding => (reference
(cpu2)) applies to receiver;
end integration.i;
```

Textual representation of a simple distributed system

Component Extensions

Component types and implementations can be extended, with the goals of reusing an existing component and adding more features (component types), subcomponent/connections (component implementations), or properties (types and implementation). Extensions are similar to object-oriented objects in their concept of inheritance. A component can only inherit from one component. If the component defines a property already defined in the parent component, the new property definition overrides the property in the parent component.

The following listing defines a new component integration2 that extends the integration component.

```
system integration2 extends integration
end integration2;
```

Defining a new component integration2

Then, we define an implementation of this system, integration2.i, that inherits the system implementation previously defined, integration.i. This new implementation contains everything from the previous

41

component but adds new elements: a new processor (cpu3), a new process (other_process), and a property association that binds them together.

```
system implementation integration2.i extends
integration.i
subcomponents
    cpu3              : processor corei7;
    other_process    : process;
properties
    actual_connection_binding => (reference
(cpu3)) applies to other_process;
end integration2.i;
```

Defining an implementation of integration2

Component Organization

Components are organized into packages, which are logical units or containers that regroup AADL declarations. You can think of an AADL package as a Java package that contains components instead of classes.

A package is defined by a name (an identifier composed of characters) and its content. You can introduce a package hierarchy by separating each namespace with two colons (::), similar to how you use the dot sign in Java. For example, aadl_book::component_definition is the correct identifier for the package component_definition inside the namespace aadl_book.

There's officially a distinction between the private and public sections, but obviously, nobody ever used the private section, which should be removed in a later version of the language.

PART 2: WHAT IS AADL?

The following example shows how to declare a package aadl_book::component_definition with two components inside: component1 and myprocess.

```
package aadl_book::component_definition
public
  system component1
  end component1;

  process myprocess
  end myprocess;
end aadl_book::component_definition;
```

Example of package and component definition

To use a package, you must include or import it. Similar to the import keyword in Java, you use the with keyword in AADL to use all the artifacts from that package. You should place this keyword after the public keyword and be sure to specify the full qualified name when using a component.

In other words, if you import the aadl_book::component_definition package, you can use it but still need to use aadl_book::component_definition::component1 to reference the component1 declaration within that package. The following example shows how to import and use the components.

```
package aadl_book::component_usage
public
  with aadl_book::component_definition
  system newcomponent component2 extends
aadl_book::component_definition::component1
  end newcomponent;

  system mysystem
  end mysystem;

  system implementation mysystem.i
  subcomponents
    c1 : system
aadl_book::component_definition::component1;
    p  : process
aadl_book::component_definition::myprocess;
  end mysystem.i;
end aadl_book::component_definition;
```

Example of components usage

AADL Property Mechanism

The property mechanism lets designers tag AADL elements (components, interfaces) to add more information such as the dispatch mechanism for a thread or the size of a data type. The general idea is to attach values that can be relevant when using the model for code generation, analysis, or just system review.

An AADL property is characterized by:
- a **unique identifier** used to name the property in models
- a **type** that defines the acceptable values. AADL properties are strongly typed, and when using them, you must define a value of this type. The AADL compiler is also strongly typed and checks the property value against the property definition.

- a **list of acceptable AADL elements** that can be assigned to the property. Certain properties make sense for some components (component category, features, etc.) but not others. For example, it would not make sense to specify the `Data_Size` of a `device`, right?

Having many checks included in the language allows for early validation of the model and component integration. By using strongly typed property values, the AADL compiler statically checks that values are being assigned correctly. It will check that boundaries are enforced (e.g., a user cannot define a temperature below 1000 if the property does not allow it) and that units are correctly used (e.g., the user cannot specify a distance in kilograms). Believe it or not, such mistakes are common and can result in safety-critical system crashes due to errors in values boundaries or unit checks.

Now, let's review how to define a property value on a component. In the following example, we associate the `Data_Size` property with the `mydata` component and specify the value of 1 bytes, which sets the size of the data type `mydata` to 1 byte. Similarly, the thread `mythr` is activated periodically every 20ms. Such properties can be used for analysis (such as scheduling) or code generation.

```
data mydata
properties
    Data_Size => 1 bytes;
end mydata;

thread mythr
properties
    Dispatch_Protocol => periodic;
    period => 20 ms;
end mythr;
```

Defining a property value

AADL defines a set of standard properties that represent properties commonly used when designing safety-critical systems. However, it is obvious that new properties are being required on a user or project basis. To satisfy this need, AADL properties can be extended, and users can introduce their own properties, as described in Part 4 of this book.

Flows

AADL introduces the concept of flows. A flow specification defines the different paths taken for transporting data from its creation to its consumption. It is the chain of elements that create, transport, process, and eventually consume the data. Think of a flow as a product chain: You create and then transport the initial product, and it's eventually consumed. The AADL flow specification is similar: There's a flow source (the producer), zero or several path (transporters), and one of several flow sinks (the consumer). Specifying the flow helps you see where data passes through the architecture.

Flow elements are specified in the textual representation in a dedicated component section called a **flow** that you specify with:

- a **unique name** to distinguish the flow inside the component and its implementation. The name of a flow implementation (in a component implementation) must be the same as the name of the flow specification (in a component type) and show how the flow is implemented.
- a **type** that explains how the data flows within this component. There are three types of flows:
  1. A flow source specifies the origination of a flow.
  2. A flow sink specifies the termination of a flow.
  3. A flow path specifies the traversal of a component.
- a **reference to a feature**: one (flow source and flow sink) or two (flow path). In the current version of AADL (AADL v2.2), flows specify logical flows with data transiting through ports. AADL v3.0 should introduce so-called hardware flows that will specify a flow with bus access passing through bus components.

Flow Specification

A component type defines flows between external interfaces (i.e., features). The same feature can be referenced in several flows. To understand the concept of flow source, flow path, and flow sink, let's review the flow definition in our previous example.

The sender components (`sender_thr` and `sender_pr`) have output ports. When looking at the component type (**and not the implementation**), these components are a `flow source`, meaning that data streams originate from them. As the component type does not define the implementation and what the component is made of, we cannot define where the data streams come from. Both components have a flow (named `f0` for `sender_thr` and `f1` for `sender_pr`) that defines the feature `valueout` as a `flow source`.

Similarly, the `receiver_thr` and `receiver_pr` components declare a `flow sink`, which they receive and consume data: it does not propagate further. Both components define a `flow sink` for the feature `valuein` (named `f4` for `receiver_thr` and `f5` for `receiver_pr`).

The `processing_thr` and `processing_pr` components transport data from their incoming port (`valuein`) to their outgoing port (`valueout`). Therefore, they define a flow path between them. Look at the `f2` flow in the `processing_thr` component: It defines a flow path between the incoming feature (`valuein`) and the outgoing feature (`valueout`). There's also a similar flow in the `processing_pr` component (flow `f3`).

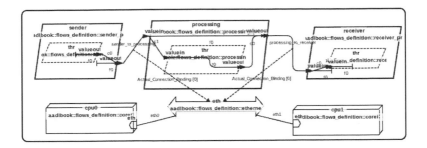

Graphical version of the model example

```
thread sender_thr
features
   valueout : out data port mydata;
flows
   f0 : flow source valueout;
properties
   Dispatch_Protocol => periodic;
period => 20 ms;
end sender_thr;


process sender_pr
features
   valueout : out data port mydata;
flows
   f1 : flow source valueout;
end sender_pr;


thread receiver_thr
features
   valuein : in data port mydata;
flows
   f4 : flow sink valuein;
properties
```

```
      dispatch_protocol => periodic;
       period => 10 ms;
   end receiver_thr;

   process receiver_pr
   features
      valuein : in data port mydata;
   flows
       f5 : flow sink valuein;
   end receiver_pr;

   thread processing_thr
   features
       valuein  : in data port mydata;
       valueout : out data port mydata;
   flows
       f2 : flow path valuein -> valueout;
   properties
       Dispatch_Protocol => periodic;
       period => 20 ms;
   end processing_thr;


   process processing_pr
   features
       valuein  : in data port mydata;
       valueout : out data port mydata;
   flows
       f3 : flow path valuein -> valueout;
   end processing pr;
```

Textual representation of an architecture using flows

Flow Implementation

A component implementation refines the flow specifications and specifies how they are implemented (thus the name flow implementation). The `flow implementation` carries out a `flow specification` and specifies how the flows use implementation elements (subcomponents, connections).

Next, let's review the concept of flow implementation using the component type `sender_pr` and its implementation `sender_pr.i`. The component type defines a flow source, `f1`, defining that its `valueout` port is a flow source. But the implementation (`sender_pr.i`) contains a thread (`thr`) and connects the `valueout` port of the thread to the `valueout` port of the process. When defining the component implementation, we can also augment the definition of flow `f1` and define how it's implemented: Flow `f1` originates in the thread and, through its flow `f0`, uses the connection `c0` to eventually reach the feature referenced in the flow definition inside the component type. We show the flow implementation for all the `process` components in our example below.

```
process implementation sender_pr.i
subcomponents
    thr : thread sender_thr;
connections
    c0 : port thr.valueout -> valueout;
flows
    f1 : flow source thr.f0 -> c0 -> valueout;
end sender_pr.i;

process implementation receiver_pr.i
subcomponents
    thr : thread receiver_thr;
connections
    c0 : port valuein -> thr.valuein;
flows
    f5 : flow sink valuein -> c0 -> thr.f4;
end receiver_pr.i;

process implementation processing_pr.i
```

```
subcomponents
    thr : thread processing_thr;
connections
    c0 : port thr.valueout -> valueout;
    c1 : port valuein -> thr.valuein;
flows
    f3 : flow path valuein -> c1 -> thr.f2 ->
c0 -> valueout;
end processing pr.i;
```

Components implementation using flows

End-to-End Flows

For now, all we have are flow elements in components without any links between them. These independent flows must be connected in some way to show how the data is transported through the architecture. We create such a connection through an end-to-end flow, which is defined in a component implementation and specifies:

- where the flow originates (the flow source)
- flow paths with connections that are used to connect them
- where the flow ends (the flow sink)

If one element is missing or specified incorrectly (e.g., a connection is missing to connect flow elements), the end-to-end flow is considered incomplete. The compiler should warn you, either when parsing the model or when instantiating the model.

To illustrate the concept of an end-to-end flow, let's review our example again. There's a flow between the sender and the receiver:

- The flow originates in the sender component.
- It traverses the processing component.

PART 2: WHAT IS AADL?

- It is finally consumed by the `receiver`.

An `end-to-end flow` is added in the `flows` section of the root component (`integration.i`) that integrates all the component together:

- It starts in the `sender` component, with the `flow` source f0.
- It uses the connection `sender_to_processing` to transport the data from the sender component to the processing.
- It passes within the `processing` component, into the flow element (`flow path`) f3.
- It uses the connection to transport the data from the `processing` component to the `receiver`.
- It is finally received by the `receiver` component, within its f5 flow element (`flow sink`).

```
system implementation integration.i
subcomponents
    cpu0      : processor corei7;
    cpu1      : processor corei7;
    sender    : process sender_pr.i;
    processing : process processing_pr.i;
    receiver   : process receiver_pr.i;
    eth       : bus ethernet;
connections
    eth0      : bus access eth <-> cpu0.eth;
    eth1      : bus access eth <-> cpu1.eth;
    sender_to_processing    : port
        sender.valueout -> processing.valuein;
    processing_to_receiver : port
        processing.valueout -> receiver.valuein;
flows

    etef0 : end to end flow
        sender.f1 -> sender_to_processing ->
```

```
    processing.f3 -> processing_to_receiver
                 -> receiver.f5;
properties
    Actual_Connection_Binding =>
    (reference (eth)) applies to
sender_to_processing,processing_to_receiver;
end integration.i;
```

End-to-end flow definition in the global system implementation

---

What's the difference between a `flow` and an `end-to-end` `flow` in a component implementation?

When declaring a flow in a component implementation, you don't have to connect a flow source to a flow sink. You just refine the flow definition from the component type and describe how the component content is used to realize the flow. In other words, you improve the accuracy of the flow definition.

When declaring an end-to-end flow, you must connect a flow source to a flow sink using other components flow elements (flow paths) and connections. In that case, you specify the flow from its origination to its termination.

The Instance Model

So far, our AADL model is made up only of components (both component types and component implementations). When using a model, you need to define your entrypoint, the top-level component of your model that's processed by analysis tools.

Using this top-level component, an instance model is generated that contains the components hierarchy and their respective elements: components, connections, flows, etc. The instance model contains everything you need to visualize or analyze your system.

So how do you create a model instance in the OSATE AADL editor? Let's create a model instance for our first example, using the steps below. The root component is the main system implementation that contains all components, integration.i.

1. To open the Outline view, click the Window menu.
2. Select the Show View and Outline options, as shown in the figure below. If Outline isn't in the list, select the Other option and search for the Outline view.

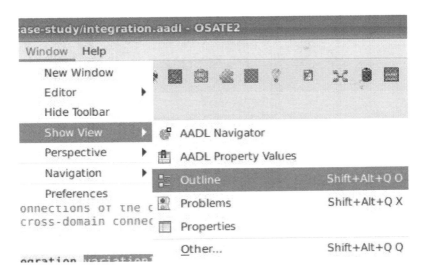

Selecting the Outline option

3. To create the system instance using `integration.i` as the root component, select the component in the Outline view of OSATE.

4. Right-click and select the Instantiate System option (see the figure below).

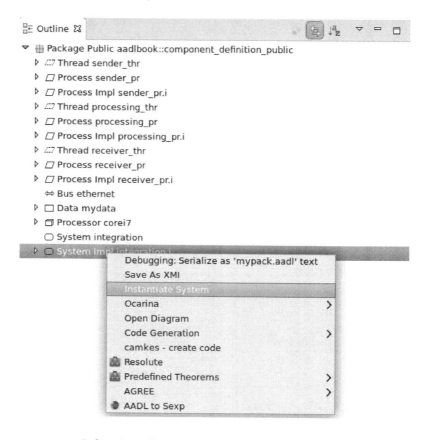

**Selecting the Instantiate System option
on the Outline view**

Creating a system instance creates a new file that contains the model instance and is located in the `instances/` directory of the same directory where the root system instance is stored. The following picture shows where the generated instance model is located.

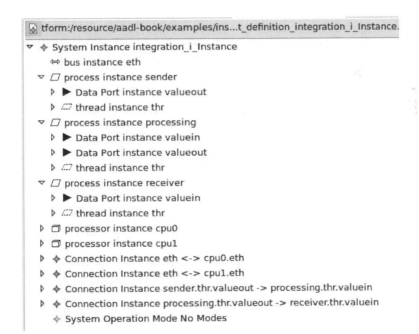

▽ 📁 > examples
　▽ 📁 > instances
　　▷ 📄 component_definition_integration_i_Instance.aaxl2

Model instance in the file explorer

You can open the file using the Eclipse Modeling Framework (EMF) editor to see the component hierarchy of the model in a single representation. Note that you can also use the property editor to visualize the property of each element.

📄 tform:/resource/aadl-book/examples/ins...t_definition_integration_i_Instance.

▽ ✦ System Instance integration_i_Instance
　　⇔ bus instance eth
　▽ ⬜ process instance sender
　　▷ ▶ Data Port instance valueout
　　▷ ⬚ thread instance thr
　▽ ⬜ process instance processing
　　▷ ▶ Data Port instance valuein
　　▷ ▶ Data Port instance valueout
　　▷ ⬚ thread instance thr
　▽ ⬜ process instance receiver
　　▷ ▶ Data Port instance valuein
　　▷ ⬚ thread instance thr
　▷ 🔲 processor instance cpu0
　▷ 🔲 processor instance cpu1
　▷ ✦ Connection Instance eth <-> cpu0.eth
　▷ ✦ Connection Instance eth <-> cpu1.eth
　▷ ✦ Connection Instance sender.thr.valueout -> processing.thr.valuein
　▷ ✦ Connection Instance processing.thr.valueout -> receiver.thr.valuein
　　✦ System Operation Mode No Modes

The model instance opened in the EMF editor

Introduction to the Case Study

Throughout this book, we illustrate how to use AADL and perform latency and safety analysis using a case study that involves an automotive system. This section presents the case study and the different AADL components that will be defined. As the book progresses, we explain how architecture elements are defined in AADL and which modeling elements and properties are relevant to the different analyses.

The code of the case study is available on a GitHub repository,[42] in the eclipse-project/case-study directory. The model is updated as the language evolves.

Presentation of a Simple Self-Driving Car

The system under consideration is a simplified self-driving car. As most readers have probably driven a car, such an example is easy to understand. The goal is not to model or analyze a complete car, and this is not an attempt to model a realistic or existing system. Modeling a complete system with a realistic architecture would introduce many components (which would require a book by itself!) and take us away from our primary objective: to apply AADL to a representative example small enough to be understandable by almost anybody. The goal of this exercise is to focus on some safety-critical characteristics and show how AADL can help to analyze them and design real-time, safety-critical systems.

---

[42]   https://github.com/juli1/aadl-book

PART 2: WHAT IS AADL?

The self-driving car system captures pictures while the car is operating in order to detect obstacles on the road. It uses two speed sensors to detect the actual car speed and initiate acceleration or braking functions. If an incoming obstacle is detected, the car initiates the brakes (with a force that will vary according to the distance the car is from the obstacle). If there is no obstacle, the acceleration function can be activated. The car also includes entertainment functions (e.g., music) and a screen that provides feedback to the passenger (e.g., actual speed, desired speed). The passenger can also set the desired speed using a panel. New cars are said to be connected and interact with the passenger's devices such as a cell phone or a tablet.

Obstacle detection and speed regulation are critical functions that must operate in a real-time, deterministic fashion. The system must satisfy these two requirements:
- **latency**
  - Upon obstacle detection, brakes are activated within 100ms and 300ms.
  - When speed changes, the acceleration or braking function is activated to reach the desired speed within 40ms to 50ms.
- **safety**
  - Failure of the entertainment system cannot result in failure of the braking and acceleration functions.
  - Speed sensors are redundant, and failure of only one speed sensor cannot prevent the car from operating.

Overview of the AADL Model

We define the AADL model using a generic system implementation (called the functional model) that is later refined into two variations that include deployment concerns. The generic model contains all common elements for both architectures. This generic model is deployment-agnostic: It defines the devices and software components (e.g., `process`) that realize the system but does not define the execution platform (e.g., `processor`, `memory`, or `bus`). All the elements of the architecture are connected and exchange the types of data defined by AADL `data` components.

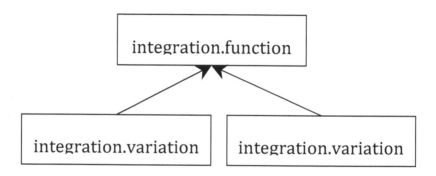

Organization of the integration model: The functional models capture all common components and extensions capture the deployment variations

Functional Model

The functional model defines the different software and hardware components used to realize the system. This case-study system follows a generic sensing/processing/actuating pattern:

1. Some sensors produce data (e.g., speed, obstacle detection).
2. The data is processed by some software components and then sent to the actuators.
3. Actuators are activated according to the data from the processing function (e.g., acceleration or brakes).

PART 2: WHAT IS AADL?

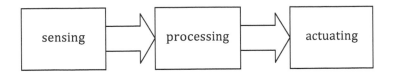

The sensing/processing/actuating architecture pattern

The following AADL components constitute the sensing functions:

- `obstacle_camera`: camera of the self-driving car (captured with an AADL `device` component). It sends the raw picture to a software component (`image_acquisition`) that detects if there is an obstacle on the road. This is a critical element.

- `obstacle_radar`: a radar that detects an obstacle on the road (specified with an AADL device component). It sends data directly to the `obstacle_detection` component, which uses processed data from the camera to detect if there is an obstacle on the road. This is a critical element.

- `wheel_sensor`: a sensor located on the wheel that indicates the vehicle speed (captured with an AADL `device` component). This is a critical element of the system.

- `laser_sensor`: another sensor that uses a laser technology to provide the vehicle speed (captured with an AADL `device` component). This sensor is redundant to the `wheel_sensor`: If the `wheel_sensor` fails, this value can be used.

- `bluetooth_ctrl`: a device that receives data from a Bluetooth bus. It interfaces with the entertainment system to control the car's music and get contacts and data from a cell phone. This is not a critical component of the system.

- `tire_pressure`: a device that transmits the tire pressure to the `panel_controller` component. This provides the ability to detect low tire pressure and send a low-pressure or flat-tire warning to the pilot. This is not a critical component.

- `panel`: a device located on the steering wheel for increasing and decreasing the speed of the car. It sends signals to the `panel_controller`, which ultimately communicates the order to the components that control the car's speed. This is not a critical component per se: If something unexpected happens (e.g., the system initiates acceleration inappropriately), the software can detect it and prevent potentially dangerous behavior.

The following components constitute the processing part of the system and rely on software components:

- `image_acquisition`: uses raw data from the camera to determine if there is an obstacle

- `obstacle_detection`: determines whether there is an actual obstacle on the road using data from `image_acquisition` and `obstacle_radar`. This component acts like a redundant/voter system with `image_acquisition`.

- `speed_voter`: receives speed from both sensors, eliminates potential bad values (due to transmission error, fault from one sensor, etc.), and outputs a consistent speed value that will be used by the speed controller and displayed on the dashboard

- `speed_ctrl`: uses the desired speed from the passenger, the actual speed, and information from the obstacle detector to appropriately initiate acceleration or braking

- `entertainment`: receives data from the Bluetooth controller (contacts and music) and sends music to play to the speaker as well as information to display on the dashboard screen
- `panel_controller`: gets information from the panel (whether the acceleration or braking function is being activated), the actual speed, and the tire pressure. Then this component produces the desired speed and information to display on the dashboard screen.

Finally, the following components represent the actuating part of the system:

- `brake`: device that applies braking to the car wheels
- `acceleration`: device that adjusts the engine and increases the vehicle's speed
- `speaker`: output of the car's sound system, where sound is produced
- `screen`: screen on the dashboard

The following picture shows the graphical representation of the AADL model, and the table below summarizes all system components with their associated type and criticality. Unfortunately, the picture is probably too big for a book and is easier to read while browsing the model using the graphical version of the model within OSATE.

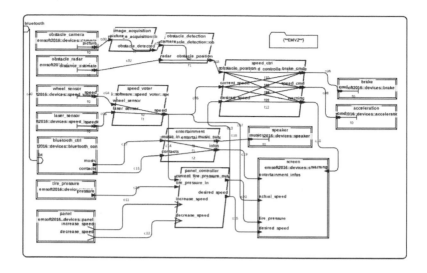

**Generic AADL model - graphical representation
(too big to be shown on a book!)**

	Component Name	Component Type	Criticality
sensors	obstacle_camera	device	high
	obstacle_radar	device	high
	wheel_sensor	device	high
	laser_sensor	device	high
	bluetooth_ctrl	device	low
	tire_pressure	device	low
	panel	device	medium
processing	image_acquisition	process	high
	speed_voter	process	high
	entertainment	process	low

Component Name	Component Type	Criticality
panel_controller	process	medium
speed_ctrl	process	high
obstacle_detection	process	high

	Component Name	Component Type	Criticality
actuators	brake	device	high
	acceleration	device	high
	screen	device	low
	speaker	device	low

System components and their type and criticality

Interfaces and Data Types

Components are connected using data ports or event ports. When communicating data, you must characterize the associated type, along with its size and other characteristics (representation, endianness,[43] etc.). Generally, all data types used to communicate between components are defined in an Interface Control Document (ICD).[44] This paragraph is a model of all data types and stands as the ICD document. All data types are defined in the aadlbook::icd package. This part of the model makes extensive use of the base_types AADL package, which defines common data types, such as integers of various size (signed/unsigned 8, 16, 32, and 64 bits) and string and floating values. The file is located in the Resources_Plugin directory, and you can open it using OSATE.

---

43 https://en.wikipedia.org/wiki/Endianness
44 https://en.wikipedia.org/wiki/Interface_control_document

PART 2: WHAT IS AADL?

We define the following types:

- obstacle_position and obstacle_position.i: capture a data structure that indicates if an obstacle is present and how far away it is. The data type is implemented as a structure with the following members:
  - present: indicates if an obstacle is present
  - x: specifies the distance from the obstacle

```
data implementation obstacle_position.i
subcomponents
   present    : data base_types::boolean;
   x          : data base_types::Unsigned_8;
end obstacle position.i;
```

Definition of the obstacle data implementation component

- speed: a 16-bit unsigned integer. We specify the number of bits using the AADL property by extending the base_types::unsigned_16 component available within the modeling environment. The base_types package is a library that contains common data types (signed/unsigned integer of 8, 16, and 32 bits, Boolean, etc.).

```
data speed extends base_types::unsigned_16
end speed;
```

Definition of the speed data type

- picture: an array of 600 Kbytes that contains the picture compressed. We use the standard AADL data_size property to specify the size of the structure and the data_model::data_representation property to specify how it's represented.

```
data picture
properties
    data_size => 600 KByte;
    data_model::data_representation => array;
end picture;
```

Definition of the picture data type

- `boolean`: a data on one bit. As for the picture, we use the `data_size` property to specify its size.

```
data boolean
properties
    data_size => 1 bits;
end boolean;
```

Definition of the Boolean data type

- `pressure`: an 8-bit integer. As for the speed, we extend a component from `base_types` to specify the constraints.
- `entertainment_infos`: an 8-bit integer. As for the speed, we extend a component from `base_types` to specify the constraints.
- `speed_cmd`: an 8-bit integer. As for the speed, we extend a component from `base_types` to specify the constraints.
- `brake_cmd`: an 8-bit integer. As for the speed, we extend a component from `base_types` to specify the constraints.
- `distance`: a 32-bit unsigned integer. As for the speed, we extend a component from `base_types` to specify the constraints.
- `music` and `music.i`: data buffers that contain audio to be played

- `contacts` and `contacts.i`: structures that contain contacts information from a cell phone

Platform Elements

Now, all functions of the system and their interaction have been defined. What needs to be defined next is how they're deployed on an execution platform (e.g., processors and buses). This section details the platform component and the association of the functional model with these platform elements. The `aadlbook::platform` package (in `platform.aadl`) defines the AADL components (AADL `processor` and `bus` components) used to deploy the software and the connections with the devices. In this package, the following elements are defined and reused later in each implementation variation:

- AADL `processor ecu`: captures a processor to execute one or more processes. This processor has two `bus accesses` that capture their connections to two AADL `bus` components. The AADL `processor` represents not only the hardware piece (the chip) but also the underlying execution software (operating system). There is an extract of the processor definition.

```
processor ecu
features
    socket1 : requires bus access can;
    socket2 : requires bus access can;
end ecu;
```

Definition of the ECU processor component

- AADL `bus can`: captures a CAN bus, a type of bus popular in the automotive domain. The CAN bus is used to transport data between devices and processors and between processes executed on different processors. We define the bus with its constraint in terms of transport capacity.

```
bus can
properties
    SEI::BandWidthCapacity => 500000.0 bitsps;
    Transmission_Time =>
        [ Fixed => 10 ms .. 30 ms;
          PerByte => 1 us .. 10 us; ];
end can;
```

Definition of the CAN bus component

Deployment Strategies

Now, all the pieces have been defined: functional architecture (devices and software) and the hardware elements that can support them. Next, we need to select the hardware elements and associate them with AADL process components and connections.

More specifically, deploying the functions consists of:
- binding AADL process components to AADL processor components to represent which chip is executing the code. Additional properties can specify certain configuration aspects (e.g., scheduling policy of the operating system).
- binding AADL process components to AADL memory components to show how they're stored in the computer memory chip and if there's a specific configuration (e.g., process stored at a particular physical address)

- associate logical AADL `ports connection` with at least one bus to represent the underlying cable and protocol being used, and the component that will physically transport the data

From a language perspective, bindings are realized with specific AADL properties that are part of the deployment_properties:

- `actual_processor_binding`: takes a reference to an AADL `processor` or `virtual processor`. This property applies to an AADL `process` or `thread`.
- `actual_connection_binding`: takes a reference of an AADL `bus` or `virtual bus`. This property applies to a `port connection`.
- `actual_memory_binding`: takes a reference to an AADL `processor` or virtual processor. This property applies to an AADL `process` or `thread` component.

Using these properties is straightforward: If you have a `processor` subcomponent `cpu` and a `process` subcomponent `pr` defined in a `system implementation` called `mysystem.i`, you declare the property in the system specification itself as follows:

```
system implementation mysystem.i
subcomponents
    cpu : processor;
    pr : process;
properties
    actual_processor_binding =>
            (reference (cpu)) applies to pr;
end mysystem.i;
```

Definition of a system implementation with processor bindings

PART 2: WHAT IS AADL?

Now that deployment mechanisms have been clarified, let's explore deployment variations.

Deployment Variation 1

The first variation uses two processors and three buses to separate the execution of software components and the allocation of connections to buses. The strategy is to separate critical functions (AADL `process` and `device` components) on different platform elements (AADL `processor` and `bus` components) and avoid sharing execution resources between functions at different criticality levels. Resources are bound as follows:

- The first processor (`cpu1`) is bound to critical parts of the system: `image_acquisition`, `speed_voter`, `obstacle_detection`, and `speed_ctrl`.

- The second processor (`cpu2`) is bound to mostly entertainment-related and non-critical software: `panel_controller` and `entertainment`.

- The first network (can1) is tied to the first processors and is bound to the following connections:
  o obstacle_camera to image_acquisition
  o obstacle_radar to obstacle_detection
  o wheel_sensor to speed_voter
  o laser_sensor to speed_voter
  o speed_ctrl to brake
  o speed_ctrl to acceleration
- The second network (can2) is associated to the second processor and transports the data from the
  o bluetooth_ctrl to entertainment
  o tire_pressure to panel_controller
  o panel to panel_controller
  o entertainment to speaker
  o entertainment to screen
  o panel_controller to screen
- The last network (can3) is associated to both processors (cpu1 and cpu2) and transports data from processes located on different processors. So, when one process that executes on cpu1 communicates with another on cpu2 (or vice versa), we bind the connection.

The following table shows the allocation of AADL process components to each component, along with their criticality.

Processor	Component Name	Component Type	Criticality
cpu1	image_acquisition	device	high
	speed_voter	device	high
	obstacle_detection	device	high
	speed_ctrl	device	high
cpu2	entertainment	process	low
	panel_controller	process	medium

AADL process components and their criticality

The following figure shows the graphical representation of the AADL model. In the textual representation, this variation is located in the `integration.aadl` file, and the related system implementation is called `integration.variation1`. As with the functional model, this is probably more readable when using the OSATE graphical modeler.

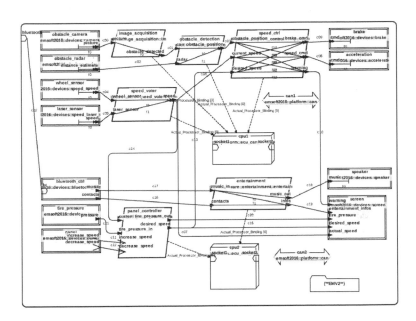

AADL version of the first deployment variation

Deployment Variation 2

The strategy of this second variation is to allocate all software processes on one processor regardless of their criticality. Doing so reduces costs as much as possible and maximizes performance (by avoiding any latency related to inter-processor communication with buses) at the cost of potential safety issues. Two CAN buses are used:

1. CAN1 transports incoming data from the sensing functions to the processing functions.
2. CAN2 transports data from the processing functions to the actuating functions.

By simplifying the footprint of the execution platform and reducing hardware components, producing this system will be cheaper. Also, a simpler footprint reduces bus connections between processors which reduces latency and increases performance. On the other hand, as all software is executed on the same processor, failure of a non-critical component might affect others at higher criticality. This is then a trade-off between cost, performance, and safety.

The following figure shows the graphical representation of the AADL model. In the textual representation, this variation is located in the `integration.aadl` file, and the related system implementation is called `integration.variation2`. As usual, reading the graphical model in a book might not be great for your eyes.

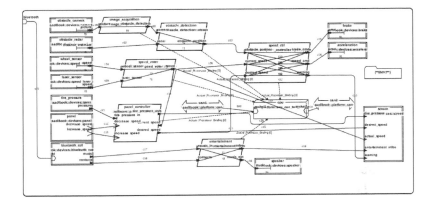

AADL version of the second deployment

Model Organization

The model is separated into several AADL packages, which increases the readability and usability of the textual version. The following packages are defined:

- `aadlbook::software` - contains all software elements. We decompose this namespace into different packages with one package for every software element:

  o `aadlbook::software::entertainment` - defines all software components for the entertainment process (thread, process, etc.)

  o `aadlbook::software::image_acquisition` - defines all software components for the `image_acquisition` process (thread, process, etc.)

  o `aadlbook::software::obstacle_detection` - defines all software components for the `obstacle_detection` process (thread, process, etc.)

75

- ○ `aadlbook::software::panel_control` - defines all software components for the `panel_control` process (thread, process, etc.)
- ○ `aadlbook::software::speed_controller` - defines all software components for the `speed_controller` process (thread, process, etc.)
- ○ `aadlbook::software::speed_voter` - defines all software components for the `speed_voter` process (thread, process, etc.)
- `aadlbook::devices:` - all devices used in the system: cameras, sensors, screens, brakes, acceleration, etc.
- `aadlbook::icd:` - all data types that realize the connections across components. This package is detailed in an earlier section.
- `aadlbook::integration:` - system implementation components that integrate the different software and hardware components as well as the two deployment variations
- `aadlbook::platform:` - platform elements (processor, bus, etc.) used to specify system deployment

Questions

1. What are the component categories of AADL?
2. What is the difference between a component type and a component implementation?
3. How does AADL capture data transfer through software?
4. What is an AADL property?
5. Can you specify an AADL thread that outputs an event named wakeup every 10 seconds?
6. Can you specify a simple software model with an AADL process bound to a processor and a memory?

Part 3: System Analysis with AADL

Part 2 introduced the core concepts of AADL as well as the self-driving-car case study (with different deployment variations) used to demonstrate analysis tools. This section shows how to use analysis tools to evaluate a model and eventually analyze each deployment variation of the self-driving-car case study. The analysis tools described below relate to latency and safety quality attributes. The main advantage is that each analysis uses different annotation mechanisms to analyze the system and thus provides a good opportunity to explore each language concept and show how it can impact the system analysis.

Latency Analysis

What Is Latency?

Latency is the time between data production and data consumption. In your car, there's a latency when you brake: a small, time gap between when you hit the brake pedal and when your car actually brakes. We want the system to be a real-time one that provides guarantees about its latency. Many people assume that whether a system is real-time somehow relates to how fast the system is running. For example, when chatting online with a friend, it is common to hear that we are communicating in real-time, but that is not what being real-time is really about,[45] especially from a safety-critical perspective. Being real-time is about determinism: an action or data will be sent or delivered in a deterministic manner at a specific time—not before and not after. After all, to avoid an obstacle on the road, your car must not turn too soon (otherwise, you might hit other cars), and it must not turn too late (otherwise, you will hit the obstacle). Your car must turn at just the right time.

Why Does It Matter?

When you see an obstacle on the road and hit the brake pedal, you want to be sure that your car actually brakes *now*—not too long before or after you press the pedal: The service (braking) has to be delivered within specified timing constraints (e.g., at the latest, within 10ms). To guarantee this timely delivery, the architect has to ensure that each component that processes the data within the latency chain will provide the requested service in a deterministic, timely manner. This is mostly the difference between safety-critical and IT systems: Most IT systems are designed with a performance, best-effort perspective in mind, while safety-critical systems must be reliable and deterministic.

Many contributors may impact the system's end-to-end latency: processor speed, shared resource (use of shared data), bus contention, jitter, execution time, and period, deadline, or scheduling protocols. Manually analyzing all these contributors is cumbersome and error-prone but necessary. And most of the time, it involves different engineers because it requires different skillsets. This is why testing (and more specifically, integration testing) is so

---

[45]   https://en.wikipedia.org/wiki/Real-time_computing

important: In the end, the designer must ensure that the system meets its deadline and the end-to-end latency is compliant with the system requirement.

Why Is an AADL-Based Model Useful for Latency Analysis?

Let's think about the factors that impact latency. Actual development processes cannot address all of them, especially early in the design process. As of today, engineers minimize latency by selecting components based on a gut feeling (also known as *empirical knowledge* or *previous successful experience*). This gut feeling is often biased and not based on objective data. Ultimately, the real validation takes place during integration testing, when it's expensive to fix such issues. If latency requirements aren't met, engineers have to change the architecture, which postpones product delivery and incurs more rework (in other words, you waste your time and money). Considering the number of factors that can increase latency, detecting the root cause can take a lot of time, and deciding to make the *right* change takes even more time (keep in mind that a change can impact other attributes and have a domino effect).

An AADL-based analysis avoids these issues because it provides a reasoning framework to analyze the system latency based on objective, unbiased metrics and offers a way to check the requirements (such as latency) and select the best alternative to realize your system. You need to model your system, but this effort pays off quickly due to all the integration issues it helps eliminate.

PART 3: SYSTEM ANALYSIS WITH AADL

Latency Modeling with AADL

In order to perform latency analysis, the model must specify:
1. the data flow from the producer to the consumer
2. all modeling element contributors that might impact system latency

This is the combination of flow specification and execution semantics (task scheduling, execution time, bus bandwidth) that allows you to estimate the end-to-end latency from the model. We first review the principles of data flow in AADL and then detail each latency contributor.

Data Flows

Latency is analyzed with regard to a particular data flow. In fact, you need to precisely know how data traverses architecture elements: where the data originates, what elements it traverses, and where it ends (which component *consumes* the data). For that reason, you need to define flow specification and implementation for each AADL component, as well as the `end-to-end flow` in AADL `component implementations` as detailed in Part 2.

Defining data flow is not enough: It just means that data is coming from an output port to an input port (and goes in different components in between). There's no interesting or meaningful information that can be used to compute the flow latency, but there are many architecture characteristics that are part of the latency contributors and can be captured with AADL.

Latency Contributors

There are two main categories of latency contributors:

- The **scheduling category**, which captures how fast components are executed and produce/consume data. This is not only a matter of execution time but rather how components are scheduled (periodic, sporadic) and if the underlying operating system enforces special policy (such as scheduling partitions using time slice). This category includes these architecture elements related to scheduling:

  o **Execution time** represents how long it takes to execute the component itself and is captured using the `Compute_Execution_Time` property in AADL `subprogram`, `thread`, or `device` components.

  o the **type of task** or more specifically, how it's activated or dispatched. A task or device is either periodic or sporadic. Periodic components are executed at a fixed rate (the period), regardless of the inputs or outputs, while sporadic components are executed only when they receive data or a signal on their input ports. This characteristic is captured using the `Dispatch_Protocol` property associated to an AADL `device` or `thread` and can take the value `periodic` or `sporadic`.

  o The **period** of a task or device specifies the execution rate of periodic components (i.e., AADL components with the `Dispatch_Protocol` property set to `periodic`) or the inter-arrival time between events for sporadic tasks (i.e., AADL components with the `Dispatch_Protocol` property set to `sporadic`). In AADL, the period is captured using the `Period` property on an AADL `thread` or `device` component with a time value.

  o the **deadline** of a task or device, which represents when the component is supposed to have completed a job and sent out the results via its output port (actions that may activate other tasks). The deadline is captured using the `Deadline` property on an AADL `thread` or `device` component.

The following code shows how to specify these properties on an AADL `thread` component:

```
thread task
properties
   --  type of task
   dispatch_protocol              => periodic;

   --  period of the task
   period                  => 10 ms;

   --  deadline of the task
   Deadline                  => 5 ms;

   --  range for the execution time
   Compute_execution_time   => 1 ms .. 2 ms;
end task;
```

Specifying the type, period, deadline, and range properties for an AADL thread component

o the **scheduling policy** of execution platforms. When tasks are executed concurrently on a shared processor, the operating system has to schedule tasks according to a specific policy. This influences the execution order of the tasks and ultimately, when new data is being produced. In AADL, the scheduling protocol is specified using the scheduling policy on AADL `processor` or `virtual processor` components, as shown in the example code below. When using an ARINC653 system, the scheduling policy is specified using the `module_schedule` property (this mechanism is detailed in the ARINC653 AADL annex).

```
processor anycpu
properties
    scheduling_protocol => (rms);
end anycpu;
```

Definition of a scheduling protocol on a processor component

Check processor bindings!

Make sure that your software components are associated (bound) with a platform. This means that your AADL `process` components must be bound to AADL `processor` or `virtual processor` components. Otherwise, analysis tools cannot take into account scheduling considerations for the latency analysis. Hopefully, in OSATE, you'll see a warning message when a `process` component is not bound.

- The **transport category** relates to how fast data is transferred between distributed nodes. When data is flowing between components located on different processors, they use buses to exchange the data. The hardware bus and transport protocols influence the end-to-end latency. These factors are related to the transport category:
  - **Bus acquisition and transmission time**: When data is being transported using a bus (AADL `connection` bound to an AADL `bus` component), two factors will impact the end-to-end latency: bus acquisition time

and transmission time. The bus acquisition time is the time required for the shared bus to be ready for transmitting data. Some buses are very non-deterministic (think about ethernet with CSMA/CD[46]), while others provide some guarantees (such as CANs that assign a priority to each node[47]). The total bus acquisition time is captured using a time range. The lower value of the range represents the best time to acquire the bus, while the higher value represents the worst time. The transmission time depends on the size of the data being transported and the bus speed (how many bytes can be transported per second). The acquisition time is captured with a range to characterize the best and worst case. These characteristics are captured using the `Transmission_Time` property on a bus component. The property is a record with two members: a `Fixed` member that characterizes the time required to acquire the link (this time does not depend on the size of the data) and a `Per_Byte` member that specifies the time required to transport a byte of data using this bus.

```
bus deterministic_bus
Properties

    --   it takes between 2 ms and 4 ms to
acquire
```

46

https://en.wikipedia.org/wiki/Carrier_sense_multiple_access_with_collision_detection

47   https://en.wikipedia.org/wiki/CAN_bus

```
  --   the bus and between 10 us and 20 us
  --   to transport a byte
  transmission_time =>
  [
    fixed   => 2 ms .. 4 ms;
     perbyte => 10 us .. 20 us;
  ];
end deterministic_bus;
```

Definition of the transmission time property on a bus component

o   A **communication protocol** also adds some time by synchronizing or organizing the data. When you surf the web, your browser relies on a full stack of protocols such as HTTP, SSL, or TCP/IP. In AADL, a protocol is captured using a `virtual bus` component, and then connections using this protocol are bound to the `virtual bus`. Finally, to capture how protocols are associated with a bus, they are also bound to a bus component. Each virtual bus (protocol) can introduce its own latency using the `latency` property.

```
virtual bus myprotocol
properties
   latency => 1 ms .. 2 ms;
end myprotocol;
```

Definition of a virtual bus with the latency property

o   The **size of the data** being transported on a bus affects the latency: The more data you have to transport, the more time you need to completely transfer it. As we mentioned earlier, the Transmission_Time property of a bus characterizes the time required to transport a byte (the PerByte member of the Transmission_Time property). This information must be used with the size of the data to compute the time necessary to transport the data from the source to the destination, so data components associated to ports (AADL event data port or AADL data port) need to specify their size. This is done with the Data_Size property from the standard property set.

```
data   integer32
properties
   data_size => 4 Byte;
end   integer32;
```

Definition of data size on a data component

Important, check connection bindings!

Make sure that your logical connections (using data port, event data port, event port) are bound to an AADL bus or virtual bus. Bindings information is used to compute the transport time between nodes. Without this information, there is no way for analysis tools to compute the transport time, which is used in many analyses such as that for latency.

The following table summarizes each latency contributor and its relevant AADL components and associated properties.

Latency Contributor	AADL Pattern
Component Execution time	`Compute_Execution_Time` property on an AADL `device`, `thread`, or `subprogram`
Dispatch Protocol	`Dispatch_Protocol` property on an AADL `device` or `thread`. The value is `periodic` or `sporadic`.
Component Period	Period property on an AADL `device` or `thread`. The value is a time value with a unit (e.g., `100ms`).
Component Deadline	Deadline property on an AADL `device` or `thread`. The value is a time value with a unit.
Processor Scheduling policy	Property on an AADL `processor` component that is scheduling the tasks. This property is specified using the `scheduling_protocol` for non-partitioning operating systems and `module_schedule` for ARINC653 systems.
Bus acquisition and transmission time	`transmission_time` property on an AADL `bus` component. This property is used for each connection bound to the related bus. `transmission_time => [ fixed => 2 ms .. 4 ms; perbyte => 10 us .. 20 us; ];`
Protocol	`Latency` property on an AADL virtual bus
Data size	`Data_Size` property on data elements associated with AADL data ports and event data ports

PART 3: SYSTEM ANALYSIS WITH AADL

Generating Latency Reports Using OSATE

It is now clear what the AADL elements of interest are for latency analysis. Next, let's review how the analysis tool works and how you use it. In a few minutes, you should be able to use the tool with our case study and also with your own models!

How Does the Tool Work?

The tools process every `end-to-end` flow declaration contained in a specific system instance. For each `end-to-end flow` declaration, the tool computes two values:

1. The **expected latency** is the value of the AADL latency property on each flow element.
2. The **actual latency** is the one computed according to the latency factors (when the task is activated/scheduled, how long it takes to transport the data, and so on).

The analysis tool computes the actual and expected latencies for each flow element of the end-to-end flow under consideration. The tool retrieves (or computes) the expected and actual latencies for each flow element of the end-to-end flow and sums them. In other words, this is how the latency is produced:

$$latency_{end\ to\ end\ flow} = \sum_{0}^{flows\ elements(end\ to\ end\ flow)} latency_{flow\ element}$$

How OSATE produces latency

Now, let's apply these principles to the case study. The `radar_to_brake` end-to-end flow defines how the data values traverse the architecture from the radar (that detects

88

obstacles on the road) to the braking device. This flow reflects the requirement that the system should brake within 100ms to 300ms if an obstacle is detected. Similarly, the `panel_to_accel` end-to-end flow checks the requirement that when speed changes, the car should accelerate or brake within 40ms and 50ms. These requirements are described in the introduction of our case study in Part 2 of this book.

In the case of the `radar_to_brake` end-to-end flow, the latency of this flow represents the time required for data from the radar to affect the braking component. In that case, when the latency analysis tool processes this end-to-end flow, it computes:

- the **expected latency** by summing up the values of the latency property of all flow segments (`obstacle_camera.f0, c00, image_acquition.f0 ... c08, acceleration.f0`)

- the **actual latency** by computing the actual latency values based on the latency contributors and AADL properties defined in the components. So the more accurate the model is, the more accurate the actual latency will be.

```
radar_to_brake : end to end flow
      obstacle_radar.f0 -> c02 ->
      obstacle_detection.f1 -> c03 ->
      speed_ctrl.f10 -> c09 -> brake.f0;
```

The `camera_to_accel` end-to-end flow definition from the camera to acceleration

Then, for each segment of the end-to-end flow and for the complete flow, the tool will show if the actual latency is higher or lower than expected. That brings two major benefits:

1. You know if the end-to-end flow actually meets your requirements.
2. If your expectations are not met and/or you want to improve your architecture and the latency, the tool points out which flow segment must be addressed.

Using the Analysis Tool

Once you have specified your data flows and the timing, scheduling, and transport characteristics, you're ready to use the latency analysis tool. To generate the latency analysis report, follow these three steps:

1. Instantiate the system.
2. Run the analysis tool on the generated system instance.
3. Locate and open the report.

Step1: Instantiate the system.

To instantiate the system, follow these steps:

1. Open the file that contains your root component (this should be a system implementation). The Outline view in Eclipse will show all component declarations.
2. Select the system implementation that represents your root component and right-click.
3. Select the Instantiate System option as shown below.

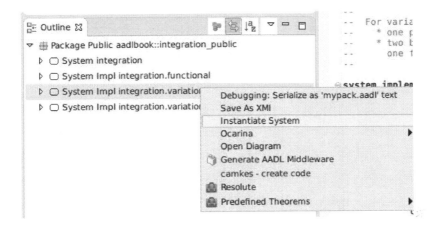

Instantiating your root system instance

Step 2: Run the analysis tool.

Once the system instance is generated, you can run the latency analysis tool on it. The generated system instance is located in a directory called `instances/`, and the file containing your instance model has the .aaxl2 extension.

PART 3: SYSTEM ANALYSIS WITH AADL

To generate the latency report, follow these steps, as show in the figure below:

1. Select the instance file and right-click.
2. Select the AADL Analyses option.
3. Select the Check Flow Latency option.

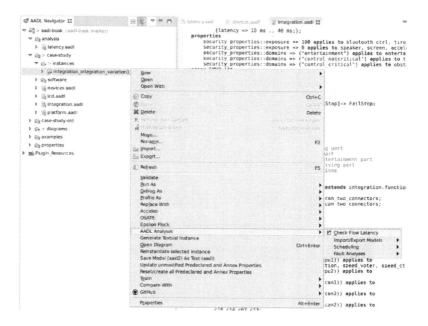

Menu to invoke the flow latency analysis

Step 3: Locate and open the analysis report.

When the flow latency analysis tool finishes, it creates two files in the `reports/latency` directory under the `instances/` directory that contains your system implementation. These reports are spreadsheets that show the latency sum for each end-to-end flow. Don't worry about the types of reports: Both contain the same information. In fact, the one with the .xls extension uses the XLS file format and contains some special formatting (e.g., background color of some cells) and can be opened with specific tools, while the one with the .csv extension is a single text file without any formatting information and can be opened with any tool.

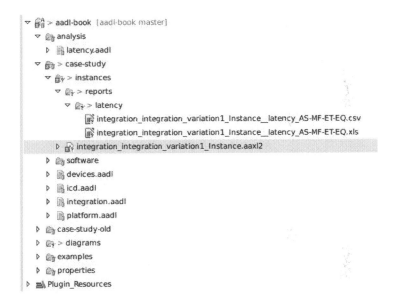

Location of the generated analysis report in the OSATE workspace

Understanding the Analysis Report

We will analyze two end-to-end flows that are related to our performance requirements:

1. **The system reacts to a change of speed within 40ms and 50ms**. We consider the end-to-end flow `panel_to_accel`, which defines a flow between the passenger panel (that sends a request to increase speed)

and the acceleration device (that receives the speed command). We define the desired latency between 40ms and 50ms by defining the latency property on this flow.

```
panel_to_accel : end to end flow
        panel.f80 -> c11 ->
        panel_controller.f99 -> c13 ->
        speed_ctrl.f22 -> c10 -> screen.f0
             {latency => 40 ms .. 50 ms;};
```

Definition of an end-to-end flow from panel to accel

2. **The system reacts to an obstacle detection within 100ms and 300ms.** We consider the end-to-end flow radar_to_brake, which defines a flow between the obstacle_radar device (that detects obstacles) and the brake device (that receives a brake command to stop the car). We associate the Latency property on this flow to specify the desired latency between 100ms and 300ms.

```
radar_to_brake : end to end flow
        obstacle_radar.f0 -> c02 ->
        obstacle_detection.f1 -> c03 ->
        speed_ctrl.f10 -> c09 -> brake.f0
             {latency => 100 ms .. 300 ms;};
```

Definition of an end to end flow from the radar to the brake

Now, let's analyze the complete list of latency contributors using the reports produced by OSATE. Note that useless rows and columns deemed unhelpful were removed in order to help you understand the results.

The first flow moves from the `panel` device to the `acceleration` device. In the first variation, as non-critical aspects and critical aspects are separated on two separate processors and connected through a bus, the flow will transit through three buses, which will increase the latency. For that reason, the latency for the first variation is between 21ms and 75ms. Unfortunately, in the worst-case scenario, requirements are not met: The latency is 75ms—greater than the required 50ms.

Contributor	Min Value	Min Method	Max Value	Max Method
(bus can1)	1.0ms	specified	1.0ms	specified
Connection	1.0ms	no latency	1.0ms	no latency
(bus can3)	10.002ms	transmission time	30.02ms	transmission time
Connection	10.002ms	no latency	30.02ms	no latency
thread speed_ctrl.accel_thr	0.0ms	sampling	5.0ms	sampling
thread speed_ctrl.accel_thr	0.0ms	no latency	5.0ms	deadline
(bus can1)	10.001ms	transmission time	30.01ms	transmission time
Connection	10.001ms	no latency	30.01ms	no latency
device acceleration	0.0ms	sampling	2.0ms	sampling
device acceleration	0.0ms	no latency	2.0ms	deadline
Latency Total	21.003ms		75.03ms	

Latency report for the end-to-end flow
`panel_to_accel` for the first deployment variation

Because the second variation doesn't separate critical and non-critical software on different processors, and executes all software on a single processor, it does not have to use an additional bus. The latency of the flow is between 16ms and 45ms, with both values under the required latency.

For the first latency requirement (the system reacts to a change of speed under 50ms), only the second variation satisfies the requirement.

Contributor	Min Value	Min Method	Max Value	Max Method
(bus can1)	1.0ms	specified	1.0ms	specified
Connection	1.0ms	no latency	1.0ms	no latency
thread speed_ctrl.accel_thr	5.0ms	sampling	5.0ms	sampling
thread speed_ctrl.accel_thr	0.0ms	no latency	5.0ms	deadline
(bus can2)	10.001ms	transmission time	30.01ms	transmission time
Connection	10.001ms	no latency	30.01ms	no latency
device acceleration	0.0ms	sampling	2.0ms	sampling
device acceleration	0.0ms	no latency	2.0ms	deadline
Latency Total	16.001ms		45.01ms	

Latency report for the end-to-end flow panel_to_accel for the second deployment variation

For the second flow, there's actually no difference because, in both cases, all software is located in the same processor. Even in the first variation, as all critical software is executed on the same processor, all connections between software components are local.

For the second latency requirement (the system reacts to an obstacle under 300ms), both system variations satisfy the requirement.

Contributor	Min Value	Min Method	Max Value	Max Method
device obstacle_radar	6.0ms	processing time	10.0ms	deadline
(bus can1)	10.001ms	transmission time	30.01ms	transmission time
Connection	10.001ms	no latency	30.01ms	no latency
thread obstacle_detection.thr	0.0ms	sampling	100.0ms	sampling
thread obstacle_detection.thr	20.0ms	processing time	100.0ms	deadline
thread speed_ctrl.brake_thr	0.0ms	no latency	5.0ms	deadline
(bus can1)	10.001ms	transmission time	30.01ms	transmission time
Connection	10.001ms	no latency	30.01ms	no latency
device brake	0.0ms	sampling	2.0ms	sampling
device brake	0.0ms	no latency	2.0ms	deadline
Latency Total	46.002ms		279.02ms	

Latency report for the end-to-end flow radar_to_brake for the first deployment variation

Contributor	Min Value	Min Method	Max Value	Max Method
device obstacle_radar	6.0ms	processing time	10.0ms	deadline
(bus can1)	10.001ms	transmission time	30.01ms	transmission time
Connection	10.001ms	no latency	30.01ms	no latency
thread obstacle_detection.thr	0.0ms	sampling	100.0ms	sampling
thread obstacle_detection.thr	20.0ms	processing time	100.0ms	deadline
thread speed_ctrl.brake_thr	0.0ms	no latency	5.0ms	deadline
(bus can2)	10.001ms	transmission time	30.01ms	transmission time
Connection	10.001ms	no latency	30.01ms	no latency
device brake	0.0ms	sampling	2.0ms	sampling
device brake	0.0ms	no latency	2.0ms	deadline
Latency Total	46.002ms		279.02ms	

Latency report for the end-to-end flow
`radar_to_brake` for the second deployment variation

Safety Analysis

When designing safety-critical systems, designers need to show that the system is reliable and resilient to different cases of failures. For that purpose, several types of analyses are necessary in order to show your system is safe and has appropriate measures to handle critical failures. Standards such as DO-178C,[48] ECSS-Q-80,[49] and ARP4761[50] define the verification activities required to analyze and validate a safety-critical system. These standards overlap each other,

---

[48]   https://en.wikipedia.org/wiki/DO-178C

[49]

   http://www.esa.int/TEC/Software_engineering_and_standardisation/TECMKDUXBQE_0.html

[50]   https://en.wikipedia.org/wiki/ARP4761

and the one you need to use depends mostly on your engineering domain.

As the objective of a MBE approach is to automate the development process, model-based tools also automate the safety validation process. The core AADL language does not support necessary language constructs to do safety analysis. For that reason, the core language was extended with an annex dedicated to safety (called the Error Model Annex v2 [AADL-EMV2]) that provides the necessary semantics for capturing safety information and showing its propagation through the architecture.

This is now a great opportunity for you to learn an annex language! The next sections introduce the main concepts of this AADL extension and explain how it can be leveraged to generate the safety reports (e.g., reports on Functional Hazard Assessment,[51] Fault Tree Analysis,[52] and Failure Modes and Effects Analysis[53]) required by standards such as the SAE ARP4761[54] (ARP4761).

Introduction to the Error Model Annex v2 (EMV2)

The Error Model Annex is an AADL extension you can use to capture what can go wrong in your architecture. The annex extends the language to specify which errors can originate from the components, how those errors propagate through the architecture, and how they might impact components' behavior.

---

[51]   https://en.wikipedia.org/wiki/Hazard_analysis
[52]   https://en.wikipedia.org/wiki/Fault_tree_analysis
[53]   https://en.wikipedia.org/wiki/Failure_mode_and_effects_analysis
[54]   https://en.wikipedia.org/wiki/ARP4761

PART 3: SYSTEM ANALYSIS WITH AADL

This annex has four levels of abstraction with level *n* depending on level *n*-1 (which means, for example, that the level-1 error flows depend on the level-0 error types ontology):

- **Level 0: error types ontology**. This list of error types distinguishes errors within the architecture and how each type, if propagated, may impact the behavior. Error types can be extended: For example, a standard `value error` can be extended by an `out of bound value error`.

- **Level 1: error flows within the architecture**. This level indicates how errors traverse the architecture, defining when errors originate (`error source`), propagate (`error path`), and impact (`error sink`) the architecture. Information at this level provides enough information to generate safety reports such as the Fault Impact report that shows how each error originating from a component (`error source`) eventually impacts the architecture.

- **Level 2: component error behavior**. This level indicates how errors impact a component's behavior: For example, is the component still operating in its nominal mode or is the component in its failure mode? The EMV2 provides the ability to attach a state machine that captures the safety component behavior according to its states, its internal failures, and errors from the outside world.

- **Level 3: composite error behavior**. Your current state might not only depend on external events but also on your subcomponents. In a hierarchical component approach like AADL, the state of the component can depend on the state of the subcomponent. For example, in our car case study, we have two different sensors for acquiring the speed of the vehicle. We might consider the system in its nominal mode when both sensors are operating and in a safe mode when only one is operating. The EMV2 provides the appropriate syntax for doing that.

The next sections detail each abstraction level and explains how it's used to analyze the system from a safety perspective.

Let's agree on terminology...at least for this book!

Some people in the AADL community argue that an error is different from a fault or failure. We recognize that language is really important and the appropriate wording should be used. However, definitions and concepts change from one community to another, making it difficult to design an annex that will satisfy all users. So let's be clear: In this book, we consider an *error* to be something that can be bad in the system and should therefore be analyzed. Some people refer to the same thing as a fault or failure. We believe the most important thing is to focus on concepts and not specific words.

Level 0: Error Types and Error Ontology

The EMV2 includes the concept of an error type. An error type is identified by a unique name that defines the error it represents: For example, the `ValueError` error type represents all errors related to the value of data.

An error type can be extended by other types, forming a complete type hierarchy. For example, the `ValueError` type can be extended by `OutOfRange` that represents when a value is not within the expected range. The `OutOfRange` error type can then be extended by `BelowRange` or `AboveRange`, which specifies how the value is out of range. Similarly, a concurrency error can be extended into a mutex error (which is then either a deadlock or starvation error) or a race condition (when a task reads or writes shared data). The picture below shows a representation of this error type hierarchy into a tree.

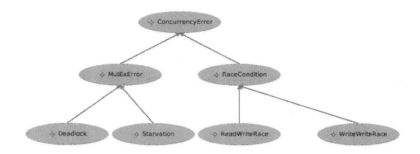

**Example of an error types hierarchy of
ConcurrencyError in ErrorLibrary.aadl**

The EMV2 defines a set of reusable error types. In OSATE, they're defined in the `ErrorLibrary.aadl` file located in the `Plugin_Resources` directory (in the Explorer view).

The predefined error types represent the common errors when designing a system. However, if the existing names and error ontology don't fit with your project, you can define your own. To do so, you need to create an AADL package with an EMV2 clause that contains your error types and extensions.

For example, let's create error types that specify the errors related to a camera. To keep it simple, only three error types are specified:

1. `CameraError`, a generic error type to indicate an error from the camera
2. `LensDirty`, which is a type of `CameraError`
3. `FocusError`, which is another type of `CameraError` specific to the Autofocus function

The error type hierarchy is shown in the following figure. The error types are defined in an AADL package that contains an EMV2 clause. The following listing shows how the errors are declared. Note that the error types are declared directly at the package level; there is no need to declare a component.

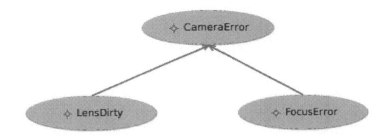

Error types hierarchy - graphical representation

```
package emv2_errortypes_definition
public

annex EMV2 {**
    error types
        CameraError : type;
        LensDirty   : type extends CameraError;
        FocusError  : type extends CameraError;
    end types;
**};

end emv2_errortypes_definition;
```

Defining an error type in an AADL file

Why are error types declared at the package level?

The answer is simple: The scope of error types (what they can be applied to) is package-wise. Error types, which should be reusable in the architecture, are not semantically limited to some components. That's why they're declared at the package level, where they can be reached by any other declaration.

Level 1: Error Flows Within the Architecture

Once we have the error types for our system, we can define how errors flow through the architecture. The EMV2 requires you to describe the following:

- **error propagations**: define which errors are coming from inside (incoming) and outside (outgoing) of the component
- **error flows**: define how incoming and outgoing error propagations relate to each other. There are three types of error flows, which mostly mimic the flows from the core standards:
  1. `error source`: specifies that the error originates within this component
  2. `error flow path`: specifies the transmission of an incoming error propagation to an outgoing error propagation
  3. `error sink`: specifies the error is stopped at this component

PART 3: SYSTEM ANALYSIS WITH AADL

Error Propagations

Error propagations specify the error types expected on component interfaces (AADL `ports`, component `provides` and `requires`) and bindings (`processor`, `memory`, or `bus`). The propagations do not define how they relate to each other; that is done with `error flows`. An error propagation is defined by:

- the name (or identifier) of the feature or binding where the error is propagated
- a direction (`in` or `out`)
- an error type set (e.g., `{ItemOmission}` or `{ValueError,ItemOmission}`)

Now, let's review how to define error propagation on one component of our case study: the camera. When this device fails, it doesn't send a picture and could potentially propagate the `ItemOmission` error type. We show this sequence of events in the following code example. Note these important lines in the EMV2 section:

1. `use types ErrorLibrary` - indicates that the component uses the types defined in this package (the one included in the regular OSATE distribution)
2. `picture: out propagation {ItemOmission}` - specifies that the `ItemOmission` error type is propagated on the picture feature. Please note that this line does not specify if the error originates from the component or if it actually just forwards it; the declaration just shows that the error is coming from the component.

```
device camera
features
    picture : out data port
aadlbook::icd::picture;
```

```
annex EMV2 {**
    use types ErrorLibrary;
    error propagations
        picture : out propagation
                  {ItemOmission};
    end propagations;
**};
end camera;
```

Error propagations for the camera component

Now, let's review the `obstacle_detection` component, which is an AADL `process` that takes the input from the camera and the radar, and produces the position of a potential obstacle on the road. This component is executed by a `processor` and expects `ItemOmission` errors on the camera's incoming ports—the one that receives data from the camera. Because the `processor` might also receive an error due to incoming or internal errors and fail to produce output, the `obstacle_detection` component also outputs the `ItemOmission` error type.

Another interesting propagation is the last one (propagation named `processor`), which specifies that the processor binding provides a `ServiceError` error type. This means that the processor bound to this `process` can propagate `ServiceError` to the `process` component. This type of error captures errors from the chip or the operating system.

```
process obstacle_detection
features
    camera : in data port
            aadlbook::icd::obstacle_position.i;
    radar  : in data port
            aadlbook::icd::obstacle_position.i;
    obstacle_position : out data port
```

```
              aadlbook::icd::obstacle_position.i;
annex EMV2 {**
    use types        ErrorLibrary;

    error propagations
        camera : in propagation {ItemOmission};
        radar : in propagation
                {ItemOmission,OutOfRange};
        obstacle_position : out propagation
                {ItemOmission};
        processor : in propagation
                {ServiceError};
    end propagations;
**};
end obstacle_detection;
```

**Error Propagations for the obstacle detection process
component**

Lastly, let's look at an example of an error propagation with the `acceleration` device. This device expects two error types on its `cmd` incoming data port: `ItemOmission` and `OutOfRange`. The `ItemOmission` error type shows that a data item is missing and that basically, an acceleration command might not be received. Similarly, the `OutOfRange` error type specifies that the command is not within reasonable range. For example, the command might ask for an acceleration increase of 2000 MPH (miles per hour), which is definitively not valid/reasonable data.

```
device acceleration
features
    cmd : in data port
aadlbook::icd::speed_cmd;
annex EMV2 {**
    use types ErrorLibrary;
```

```
    error propagations
        cmd : in propagation
                        {ItemOmission,OutOfRange};
    end propagations;
**};
end acceleration;
```

Error propagation for the acceleration component

Error Flows

Error propagations specify what error types components are expected to send or receive. But it does not specify how incoming and outgoing error types relate to each other: Nobody can know how an error type from an incoming port can eventually generate an error type on an outgoing port or how an error from the `processor` might affect a process and result in an outgoing propagation on its data ports. The relationship between error types is defined with `error flows`, which are extensions of error propagations. Error flows follow a construction similar to flows from the core language.

An error flow can be:
- an `error source`: The error originates from or within the component. The component has an internal failure that will eventually generate the error being propagated.
- an `error path`: The error is propagated by the component, passing it from an incoming error propagation to an outgoing one.
- an `error sink`: The error is handled and/or mitigated in a component.

An error flow specification is composed of the following elements:

- a **unique identifier**
- the **type of error flow** (i.e., error source, error path, or error sink)
- the **name of the referenced error propagations and associated error types**. For `error source` and `error sink`, only one error propagation is required (`outgoing` for `error source`, `incoming` for `error sink`). For error path, two propagation paths are required (separated by the arrow sign [`->`]): one for the incoming error propagation and another for the outgoing error propagation.

Next, let's review the definition of an error flow on the camera system from the use case. The camera can have an internal error that will eventually propagate the `ItemOmission` error type (meaning some data will not be sent) and that is an `error source` for the `ItemOmission` error type. In the following code, we declare this error flow with the `ef0` identifier:

```
device camera
features
    picture : out data port
                    aadlbook::icd::picture;
annex EMV2 {**
    use types ErrorLibrary;

    error propagations
        picture : out propagation{ItemOmission};
    flows
        ef0 : error source
                    picture{ItemOmission};
    end propagations;
**};
end camera;
```

Error propagations and flows for the camera

Now, let's review how to define an error path. The `obstacle_detection` component has incoming and outgoing errors that relate to each other: An error from the camera data will eventually impact the detection of an obstacle, and failure from the processor will also impact this outgoing data. We capture this error propagation dependency in the `ef0`, `ef1`, and `ef2` error flows:

- `ef0`: The error flow specifies that an `ItemOmission` from the camera is ultimately passed as an `ItemOmission` error type on the outgoing `obstacle_position` error propagation.

- `ef1`: The error flow specifies that an `ItemOmission` from the radar is ultimately passed as an `ItemOmission` error type on the outgoing `obstacle_position` error propagation.

- `ef2`: The error flow specifies that a `ServiceError` from the associated processor (the one executing the process) is ultimately passed as an `ItemOmission` error type on the outgoing `obstacle_position` error propagation.

In an error path, the incoming error type can match the outgoing error type (as in `ef0` and `ef1`), but it does not have to (as in `ef2`). For example, a `ServiceOmission` from a processor can be transformed as an `ItemOmission` on the outgoing features of the processes it executes. In other words, you can transform the error types from incoming to outgoing error propagation.

```
process obstacle_detection
features
    camera : in data port
            aadlbook::icd::obstacle_position.i;
```

```
  radar  :  in data port
          aadlbook::icd::obstacle_position.i;
   obstacle_position  :  out data port
          aadlbook::icd::obstacle_position.i;
annex EMV2 {**
  use types ErrorLibrary;

  error propagations
     camera  :  in propagation
                {ItemOmission,OutOfRange};
     radar  :  in propagation
                {ItemOmission,OutOfRange};
     obstacle_position  :  out propagation
                {ItemOmission};
     processor  :  in propagation {ServiceError};
  flows
     ef0  :  error path camera{ItemOmission} ->
obstacle_position{ItemOmission};
     ef1  :  error path radar{ItemOmission} ->
obstacle_position{ItemOmission};
     ef2  :  error path processor{ServiceError} ->
obstacle_position{ItemOmission};
  end propagations;
**};
end obstacle_detection;
```

**Error propagations and flows
for the obstacle_detection component**

Lastly, let's review how to declare an `error sink`, such as the `acceleration` device. The `cmd` incoming feature is associated with the `ItemOmission` and `OutOfRange` error types. This component is ultimately impacted by these errors (whether the component manages/handles the error is a different issue). From an architecture perspective, this is an `error sink` that we specify in the `ef0 error flow` below. Note that when specifying error propagation and error flows, we can specify more than one error type and, in fact, can associate sets of error types. The following example

111

shows how to use the syntax to specify two error types (`ItemOmission` and `OutOfRange`):

```
device acceleration
features
    cmd : in data port aadlbook::icd::speed_cmd;
annex EMV2 {**
    use types ErrorLibrary;

    error propagations
    cmd : in propagation
                {ItemOmission,OutOfRange};
    flows
        ef0 : error sink
                cmd{ItemOmission,OutOfRange};
    end propagations;
**};
end acceleration;
```

Error propagations and flows from the acceleration component

Consistency between error behavior and error flows

Both `error propagations` and `error flows` use error types to describe the types being propagated or handled within the component. It is important to make sure your specification is consistent: Error types in the flows sections must be referenced in the propagations section. If the error types in the flows are not in the propagations, the error specification is said to be inconsistent. The modeling tools should verify the model consistency automatically. OSATE and its EMV2 extensions do this verification automatically, showing errors in the textual editors for any consistency issues.

PART 3: SYSTEM ANALYSIS WITH AADL

Level 2: Component Error Behavior

The next level of abstraction is the `error behavior state machine` (EBSM). It allows you to associate a safety-specific state machine with a component that precisely defines the component state according to `incoming error propagations` and internal `error events`. In the Error Model Annex, the specification of the EBSM is made in two passes:

1. First, a generic state machine is specified that is completely component-agnostic and can be associated with any other component.
2. Then, the designer refines the generic state machine to match the specifics of the component (incoming/outgoing error propagations, internal error events, etc.).

Why have different types of error behavior state machines?

You might wonder why we have different state machines and bother to have a generic one. Wouldn't it be simpler to just specify the EBSM in the component? That could be a solution, but as many components use the same behaviors, it is more efficient to factor all state machines in a single location and share them across components. However, some adaptation is always needed when we integrate the EBSM with a component. For example, defining the transition and change of state according to incoming ports can be done only when we are in the scope of the component.

Generic Error Behavior State Machine

PART 3: SYSTEM ANALYSIS WITH AADL

EBSMs are defined in EMV2 subclauses of AADL packages and then assigned and refined within components.

First, we need to define the generic state machine in AADL packages. In OSATE, the `ErrorLibrary.aadl` file in the `Plugin_Resources` project already declares some generic state machines. As error types, generic state machines are declared in a package so that they can be reused by any other component.

A generic behavior state machine is defined by:
- a unique identifier (basically, a name that can be referenced within the modeling environment)
- zero to several `error event(s)` that represent internal errors inside the system. Each event is identified with a unique name within the component.
- one or more `error state(s)` with exactly one initial state. An `error state` is defined by a unique name within the state machine.
- one or more `error transition(s)`. An `error transition` is defined by a unique name, a starting state, a condition, and a resulting state.

Let's review the `FailStop` state machine defined in the `ErrorLibrary.aadl` file (in the `Plugin_Resources` directory). This state machine has one `error event` named `Failure` and two states: `Operational` (initial state) and `FailStop`. One transition changes the state from operational to `FailStop` when the `Failure` event arises.

```
error behavior FailStop
events
    Failure     : error event;
states
```

```
    Operational : initial state;
    FailStop    : state;
transitions
    FailureTransition : Operational
                      -[ Failure ]-> FailStop;
end behavior ;
```

The FailStop state machine – EMV2 textual representation

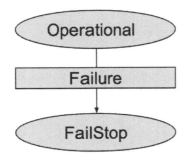

The FailStop state machine - graphical representation

The FailStop EBSM has only one transition, and basically, when you're in the FailStop state, you never get back: You stay stuck in this state. A component like this will operate until a failure happens and a reset event needs to be triggered. Many systems have recovery events that let them recover from a failure and that we can capture with a recover event. Let's review the FailAndRecover state machine, also available in the ErrorLibrary.aadl file, that implements such a behavior. This state machine has one error event (Failure) and one recover event (Recovery) that triggers a recovery error from a failure

115

state. The state machine has two states: Operational and Failed. As for the FailStop state machine, there's a transition from the Operational state to the Failed state when a failure happens. The other transition moves the system from the Failed to Operational state.

```
error behavior FailAndRecover
events
    Failure: error event;
    Recovery: recover event;
states
    Operational: initial state;
    Failed:   state;
transitions
    FailureTransition :
        Operational -[ Failure ]->Failed;
    RecoveryTransition :
        Failed -[ Recovery ]->Operational;
end behavior;
```

The FailAndRecover State Machine

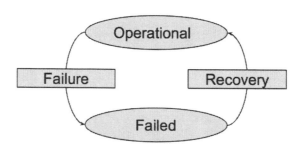

The FailAndRecover state machine - graphical representation

Association with a Component

Once the generic EBSM is associated with a component, we can extend the state machine with other error events and transitions. Let's review the behavior of the acceleration device—a component that uses the `FailStop` EBSM that we defined before. You associate the state machine with the component using the `use behavior` statement in the EMV2 subclause.

Where are transitions and error events defined?

We can define events and transitions in the EBSM or in the `component error behavior` associated with the components. There is no obvious rule about where to define them; it's a matter of choice and taste.

For example, in the previous sections, we introduced the `FailStop` and `FailAndRecover` state machines and argued that we needed the `FailAndRecover` to model the `recover` event. Another way of adding the `recover` `event` (and its associated transitions) is to put it in the component error behavior of its associated component. The good news is the language is pretty flexible. I recommend defining your own modeling guidelines and sticking to them!

In the `component error behavior` section, we extend the state machine with other `error events` and `error transitions`. We also specify how incoming `error propagations` impact the `component error behavior state`. For the `acceleration` device, we add the following:

- a recover event with the `Reset` identifier

- a transition (t0) that changes the state from Operational to FailStop when the ItemOmission error type is received on the cmd incoming feature
- a transition (t1) that changes the state from Operational to FailStop when the OutOfRange error type is received on the cmd incoming feature
- a transition (t2) that changes the state from FailStop to Operational when the Reset recover event is triggered

```
device acceleration
features
  cmd : in data port aadlbook::icd::speed_cmd;
annex EMV2 {**
  use types          ErrorLibrary;
  use behavior       ErrorLibrary::FailStop;

  error propagations
    cmd : in propagation
                  {ItemOmission,OutOfRange};
  flows
    ef0 : error sink
          cmd{ItemOmission,OutOfRange};
  end propagations;

  component error behavior
  events
    Reset : recover event;
  transitions
    t0 : Operational
            -[cmd{ItemOmission}]-> FailStop;
    t1 : Operational
            -[cmd{OutOfRange}]-> FailStop;
    t2 : FailStop -[Reset]-> Operational;
  end component;
**};
end acceleration;
```

Error behavior state machine of the acceleration device

So now, the EBSM of the acceleration component looks like the one in the figure below. There are the original states and transitions from the generic `FailStop` state machine, as well as the additional events and transitions specific to the `acceleration` component.

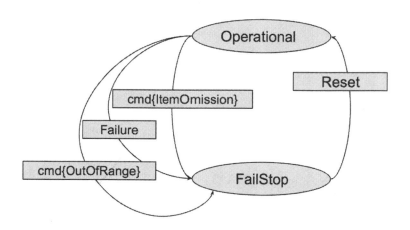

The complete error behavior state machine of the acceleration component

Completeness of the state machine
How complete is your state machine? Is there any non-determinism? Did you cover all potential combinations of events? Depending on what type of system you're developing, you might want to consider potential non-deterministic behaviors. For example, you want to make sure that the condition of each transition references each incoming error propagation and error event. Another validation is to check that each state has at least one transition. It is really important to check that the

specification is complete and unambiguous. The EMV2 tools integrated in OSATE have plug-ins that verify the consistency of your error model and detect potential issues related to determinism.

Level 3: Composite Error Behavior

The EBSM provides a way to specify the error behavior for a component with its inputs and outputs. However, in this state machine, we cannot represent the state of a component according to its subcomponents. In some cases, your state (e.g., `Operational`, `Failed`) does not depend on inputs or outputs but rather on the state of your subcomponents. For example, if you have a system that provides the temperature from two redundant sensors, you might want to specify the state of your system according to the state of the subcomponents. When all sensors are working, the system will be in the operational mode. When only one sensor is active and operating, the whole system would be considered in a degraded mode, and if no sensor is active, the system will be in the failed state.

You indicate the current state according to your subcomponent through a `composite error behavior`, which can be specified only in the component implementation where subcomponents are specified.

A `composite error behavior` requires the inclusion of a `generic error behavior state machine` that defines the `error states` of your component. Then, you must logically define the component `error state` according to the `error states` of its subcomponent.

120

The composite error behavior is also useful when defining the error states of the root component that integrates all the components together. For example, for the top-level component of our car system, we use a composite error behavior to define the failure conditions of the system. The following listing illustrates the composite error behavior of the integration.functional component: The system is in the FailStop state when both the brake **and** the acceleration components are in the FailStop state.

```
system implementation integration.functional
--
--    all subcomponents
--    and properties declaration
--
annex EMV2 {**
    use types        ErrorLibrary;
    use behavior     ErrorLibrary::FailStop;

    composite error behavior
    states
        [brake.FailStop and
        acceleration.FailStop]-> FailStop;
    end composite;
**};
end integration.functional;
```

**Specification of the composite error behavior
of the integration.functional component**

Error Properties

As for the core language, the Error Model Annex also defines its own property mechanism. The goal is to annotate the EMV2 elements (error propagation, flow, states) with information that can be used by model analysis tools.

PART 3: SYSTEM ANALYSIS WITH AADL

The EMV2 properties are declared into a properties section in the EMV2 subclause.

The following properties are used for the safety analysis available in OSATE:

- **emv2::occurrencedistribution**: specifies the occurrence of an error event or error propagation. It defines the distribution function of the error and its associated value.

- **emv2::severity**: the severity of an error event or error propagation. It is a number from 1 (high) to 5 (low). In order to comply with the wording used in certification standards, OSATE includes constants to use the label from the standard (e.g., ARP4761,[55] MIL-STD 882D[56] [MIL-882D]).

- **emv2::likelihood**: the likelihood for an error event or error propagation to occur. The value is a literal ranging from A (high) to E (low). Standards like ARP4761 or MIL-STD 882D have different wording, and OSATE provides property constants to adapt to the appropriate wording.

- **emv2::hazards**: specifies additional information associated with an error event, error state, or error propagation. The property captures all data used by safety analysis that requires the extraction of information from any occurring error. The property is a record that requires fields such as title, failure description, failure effect, mission phases, verification method, etc.

---

55   https://en.wikipedia.org/wiki/ARP4761
56   https://en.wikipedia.org/wiki/United_States_Military_Standard

The example below illustrates how to define properties for the EMV2 elements of the camera component. We define the properties emv2::occurrencedistribution, emv2::severity, emv2::likelihood, and emv2::hazards. The focus here is the definition of properties on the error propagation for the picture feature, when it propagates the ItemOmission error type. We associate a likelihood, a severity, an occurrence, and hazards.

```
device camera
features
 picture : out data port
                  aadlbook::icd::picture;
annex EMV2 {**
 use types        ErrorLibrary;

 error propagations
  picture : out propagation {ItemOmission};
 flows
  ef0 : error source picture{ItemOmission};
 end propagations;

 properties
  emv2::occurrencedistribution => [
       probabilityValue => 0.01e-4 ;
       Distribution => Poisson;]
            applies to picture.itemomission;
  emv2::severity => ARP4761::Major
            applies to picture.itemomission;
  emv2::likelihood => ARP4761::Probable
            applies to picture.itemomission;
  emv2::hazards =>
   ([   crossreference => "N/A";
        failure        => "ItemOmission";
        phases         => ("all");
        description    =>
               "No picture from the camera";
        comment        =>
```

```
                    "Would impact the detection of
        obstacle if the radar is not working as well";
                ])
                applies to picture.itemomission;
    **};
    end camera;
```

Camera component with EMV2 properties

For the severity and likelihood, we do not associate a value (integer or literal) but rather a constant with the prefix ARP4761. This is due to the way that EMV2 machinery defines property constants and tries to follow the wording of the certification standard. While the EMV2 standard document expects an integer or a literal for the severity or likelihood, certification standards, such as ARP4761 or MIL-STD 882D, use words instead. For example, for severity, ARP4761 uses the words catastrophic, major, and minor, while EMV2 uses frequent, probable, remote, and extremelyimprobable. To make using the annex easier and have wording as close as possible to the existing standard, EMV2 defines property constants that map the ARP4761 wording to EMV2 values.

The following code shows how it's done internally. In fact, ARP4761::Major is a property constant whose value is 3. Then, declaring

```
        emv2::severity => ARP4761::Major
```

is the same thing as declaring

```
        emv2::severity => 3
```

124

The EMV2 tools use the same mechanism to map likelihood labels and provide the same mapping rules for the MIL-STD-882 standard.

```
property set ARP4761 is
    with EMV2;
    -- Severity labels: for EMV2::Hazards
    -- and EMV2::Severity
    Major : constant EMV2::SeverityRange => 3;

    -- Likelihood labels for EMV2::Hazards
    --   and EMV2::Likelihood

    Probable : constant
              EMV2::LikelihoodLabels => B;
    -- other declarations
end ARP4761;
```

Declarations of constants for ARP4761

Annotating the Car Model

The AADL model of the case study needs to be annotated to perform safety analysis. Our case study follows a sensing, processing, and actuating pattern. In such a pattern:

- **Sensing elements** are producing new data. Because they can generate new errors, they can be an error source.
- **Processing elements** are either propagating errors (error flows), generating errors (error source), or mitigating errors (error sink).
- **Actuating elements** are impacted by errors and may define a strategy for error mitigation or recovery (error sink).

In this architecture, we focus on the following error types:

- `ItemOmission`: A data element has not been sent.
- `OutOfRange`: The data value is out of range due to a computation error, bit flip, etc.
- `ServiceError`: The service is not provided as expected. We use this error type for the processor that executes the software.

Almost all components that belong to the sensing domain are an `error source` for one or both `error types` (`ItemOmission` and `OutOfRange`).

Similarly, most of the components from the processing domain are `error path` and transmit error from their input ports to their output ports. We noticed some error type transformation, like in the `speed_ctrl` component where:

- An incoming `ItemOmission` error is transformed into an `OutOfRange` error. If the incoming element is not coming (`ItemOmission`), the process might then send an incorrect previous value and/or some value taken from an uninitialized memory area (`OutOfRange`).
- A `ServiceError` (from the bound processor) is transformed into an `ItemOmission`. In fact, if the processor is not working correctly (`ServiceError`), it will impact the process it executes, and no data will be sent (`ItemOmission`).

Finally, components from the actuating domain are `error sinks` that handle, mitigate, or are impacted by the error. Regardless, this is where the `error flow` ends.

We also define an EBSM on the acceleration and brake components, which use the `ErrorLibrary::FailStop` behavior state machine and extend it. For any of them, if one `ItemOmission` or `OutOfRange` is received on the

components' interfaces, the component switches to the
FailStop state. The definition of the components is shown
below:

```
device brake
features
 cmd : in data port aadlbook::icd::brake_cmd;
annex EMV2 {**
 use types    ErrorLibrary;
 use behavior ErrorLibrary::FailStop;

 error propagations
  cmd : in propagation
            {ItemOmission,OutOfRange};
 flows
  ef0 : error sink cmd
            {ItemOmission,OutOfRange};
 end propagations;

 component error behavior
 events
  Reset : recover event;
 transitions
   t0 : Operational
            -[cmd{ItemOmission}]-> FailStop;
   t1 : Operational
            -[cmd{OutOfRange}]-> FailStop;
   t2 : FailStop    -[Reset]-> Operational;
 end component;
**};
end brake;

device acceleration
features
 cmd : in data port aadlbook::icd::speed_cmd;
annex EMV2 {**
 use types    ErrorLibrary;
 use behavior ErrorLibrary::FailStop;

 error propagations
```

```
    cmd : in propagation
              {ItemOmission,OutOfRange};
  flows
   ef0 : error sink cmd
          {ItemOmission,OutOfRange};
   end propagations;

   component error behavior
   events
     Reset : recover event;
   transitions
    t0 : Operational
          -[cmd{ItemOmission}]-> FailStop;
    t1 : Operational
          -[cmd{OutOfRange}]-> FailStop;
    t2 : FailStop
          -[Reset]-> Operational;
   end component;
**};
end acceleration;
```

The brake and acceleration devices with the definition of their behavior state machine (properties and flows from the core language have been removed)

Finally, we define the error behavior of the top component, integration.functional, with a composite error behavior that defines the failure condition of the entire system. In fact, the condition is very straightforward: The system fails if the acceleration and the brake components are both in the FailStop state (i.e., they are both failing). Note that there is no end-to-end error flow (whereas there are end-to-end flows in the core language): error flows follow the logical connections within the system implementation.

```
system implementation integration.functional
annex EMV2 {**
  use types          ErrorLibrary;
  use behavior       ErrorLibrary::FailStop;

  composite error behavior
  states
    [brake.FailStop and
      acceleration.FailStop]-> FailStop;
  end composite;
**};
end integration.functional;
```

Specification of the composite error behavior of the integration.functional component showing that the main system is failing if the brake and acceleration are failing

The model is now fully annotated with error information and ready to be processed by safety analysis tools to generate safety analysis reports.

Safety Analysis Tools

Functional Hazard Assessment

The Functional Hazard Assessment[57] (FHA) is a safety analysis mandated by the ARP4761[58] [ARP4761] safety standard. The FHA is a comprehensive analysis of all functions to identify exceptional conditions that may trigger an error. The ARP4761 standard provides a list of possible severities to classify those conditions. In AADL terms, we

---

[57]   https://en.wikipedia.org/wiki/Hazard_analysis
[58]   https://en.wikipedia.org/wiki/ARP4761

consider that a function is specified by an AADL component (regardless of the associated component type). An exceptional condition and then hazard would be an EMV2 artifact such as an `error event` or an `outgoing error propagation` specified as an `error source`.

The analysis tool scans each component and reports information about all the `error events` and `error sources` on it. In order to capture the severity, description, and so on, the following EMV2 properties must be defined on the relevant EMV2 artifacts to be included in the analysis report:

- `Emv2::occurrencedistribution` defines the occurrence of the hazard.
- `Emv2::severity` defines the severity, as defined by the ARP4761 or MIL-STD-882 [MIL-882D].
- `Emv2::likelihood` defines the likelihood as defined by the ARP4761 or MIL-STD-882 [MIL-882D].
- `Emv2::hazards` provides information (comments, description) about the hazard.

Once the analysis is done, the analysis tools generate a spreadsheet that contains the list of all hazards with the information that has been gathered from the models (through the properties).

How Do You Use the Analysis?

To use the analysis, you must first instantiate your system using the steps below:

1. Select a system implementation in the Outline view of OSATE and right-click.
2. Select the Instantiate System option, as shown in the figure below. Then, in the `instances/` directory,

OSATE will create a new file that contains the instance model the analysis will run against.

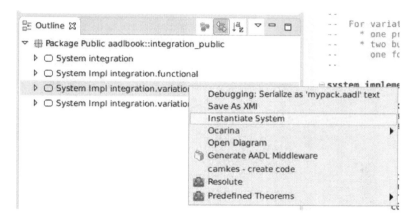

Instantiate the system implementation first

To run the analysis tool against the new system instance, select the instance file and invoke the Functional Hazard Assessment function as follows:

1. Click on the Analyses menu.
2. Select the Fault Analyses option.
3. Select the Functional Hazard Assessment option.

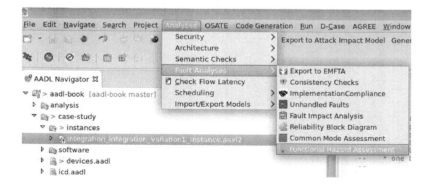

PART 3: SYSTEM ANALYSIS WITH AADL

Select the system instance and invoke the analysis tool

Once the analysis is completed, the analysis report is available under the `instances/reports/FHA` subdirectory, as shown below. The result of the FHA analysis is a comma separated values (CSV)[59] file that can be opened with any modern spreadsheet system such as Libreoffice[60] (most commercial productivity suites also support this format).

---

[59] https://en.wikipedia.org/wiki/Comma-separated_values
[60] https://www.libreoffice.org/

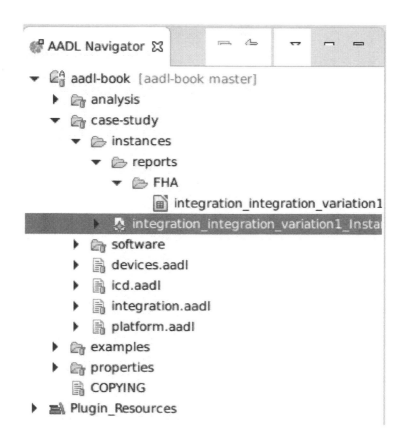

**The location of the generated FHA report
(shown in the Explorer view of OSATE)**

To open the file, follow these steps:
1. Select the file and right-click.
2. Select the Open option. The following picture shows the FHA created for our example in Libreoffice.

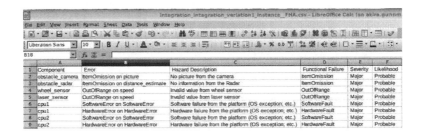

The generated FHA report in LibreOffice

Fault Tree Analysis

The Fault Tree Analysis[61] (FTA), which shows the hierarchy of `errors events` and `error sources` related to a particular `error state`, is more complex because it relies on more modeling elements than the FHA.[62] The FHA lists all potential errors for the system, while the FTA shows the dependencies between error events and error propagation related to a special condition. For this reason, the FTA is a better way to analyze a particular `error event`.

The following picture shows a generic fault tree that details the conditions for a failure with a computer: The computer crashes if one or more of these conditions are met:

- An unhandled interrupt is raised.
- A device breaks (e.g., the internal clock).
- A software error occurs due to both of these conditions:
  - A divide by zero occurs.
  - There is no handler for such an exception.

---

61   https://en.wikipedia.org/wiki/Fault_tree_analysis
62   https://en.wikipedia.org/wiki/Hazard_analysis

Of course, this small example is not exhaustive but basically shows you what an FTA is and its hierarchical nature. Note that the FTA is made up of the following elements:

- **error events:** notice a state of the system or also that "something happened." There is at least one event in the FTA—the root event. In the case of our example, the root event is a computer crash. When error events are not leaves, they're associated with a gate that defines the condition that raises the error event. Our example has the following leaves:
  - device broken
  - unhandled interrupt
  - divide by zero
  - no recovery handler
- **gate:** When the error event is not a leaf, the gate defines the condition that raises an event. The condition is a binary condition such as OR, AND, or XOR. In our example, there are two gates: one under the "computer" event and one under the "software" event.

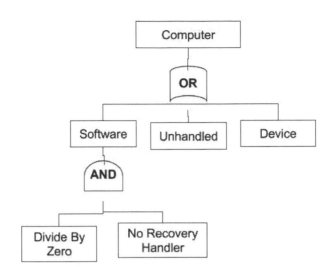

Example of a fault tree

While this example is small and not representative of a realistic system, it should be enough to help you understand the concept of a fault tree. Certifying safety-critical systems in avionics or aerospace domains requires the creation of a fault tree from design documents written in natural languages. Such a fault tree contains thousands of error events and gates. Needless to say, ensuring that the FTA is consistent with all development artifacts is error-prone and difficult. This is where AADL comes to the rescue and can ultimately automate the production of the FTA from the architecture model (which could ultimately be the specification).

When generating fault trees from AADL models, the following EMV2 elements are relevant:

- **error propagations and error flows:** The FTA[63] analysis tool will search for `error sources` and `error events` that impacted the component under analysis.

- **error behavior state machine:** The EBSM of all components connected to the component under analysis. The tool detects the `error events` or `error propagations` that can impact the component under analysis. For example, if a particular component propagates an `error type` only when being in a particular state, then all `error sources` or `error events` that switch the components to this state will be a contributor.

- **composite error state machine:** The `composite error state` machine defines the `error state` of a component according to the `error states` of its subcomponents. This definition is an essential element of the FTA, and the system instance must have a `composite error state machine` that initiates the FTA. The analysis starts with the final state of the system instance and processes the states of the subcomponents referenced in the `composite error behavior`.

- **EMV2::occurrencedistribution property:** The `occurrencedistribution` property is used to complete the FTA diagram with the appropriate probabilities. The FTA tool can then use these values to compute the probability of a failure or show the probability of each cutset.

How Does the FTA Generation Algorithm Work?

---

63   https://en.wikipedia.org/wiki/Fault_tree_analysis

PART 3: SYSTEM ANALYSIS WITH AADL

The algorithm that generates an FTA diagram starts with a component C and an error state S; for example, the component `integration.implementation1` is in the `FailStop` error state.

The tool then calls the `generateFTA (C, S)` function, which returns an FTA error event and works as follows:

1. It analyzes the `composite error state` machine of the C component and S state. For every expression where C is in the S error state, the algorithm processes the condition elements, and for each referenced C2 subcomponent and S2 state, it applies the algorithm recursively for C2 and S2, calling `generateFTA (C2, S2)`. Each generated event is then added to the tree. When processing the condition, the algorithm enforces the condition logic and maps and/or logic into AND/OR gates. If there are multiple composite error state statements for S in C, each is processed, and the results are put under an OR gate.

2. It analyzes the EBSM of component C and looks for any transition that caused the component to transition into S. If one or more transitions to S exist, all are processed, and their results are put under an OR gate. The condition logic (AND/OR) is preserved and mapped into an AND/OR gate. Then:

   a. If the condition references an `error event`, the event is mapped to an `error event` and added to the FTA. Its probability is pulled from the `EMV2::occurrencedistribution` property.

   b. If the condition references an `incoming error propagation`, the algorithm follows the propagation paths (along AADL `connections`) and analyzes the C3 component that initially propagates the error (i.e., the component with the related `error source` that triggers the incoming `error propagation` in C) and then:

i. If the error source is only propagated when the component is under a certain S3 state, the algorithm is recursively called with C3 and S3 (i.e., calling `generateFTA (C3, S3)`).

ii. Otherwise, the error source is added as an `error event` in the FTA. Probabilities of the error sources are retrieved from the `EMV2::occurrencedistribution` property.

This algorithm creates the fault tree from an AADL model. The actual code for this is provided in the EMV2 analysis tools on GitHub[64] and in the EMV2 support. In particular, the algorithm is mostly implemented into the PropagationGraphBackwardTraversal[65] class. The EMFTAGenerator[66] class extends this class and implements all the EMFTA-specific aspects.

How Do You Use the FTA Analysis?

---

[64]

https://github.com/osate/ErrorModelV2/tree/develop/org.osat e.aadl2.errormodel.analysis/src/org/osate/aadl2/ errormodel/analysis/fta

[65]

https://github.com/osate/ErrorModelV2/blob/develop/org.osat e.xtext.aadl2.errormodel/src/org/osate/xtext/ aadl2/errormodel/util/PropagationGraphBackwardTraversal.java

[66] https://github.com/cmu-sei/emfta/blob/develop/org.osate.aadl2.errormodel.emfta/src/org/o sate/aadl2/ errormodel/emfta/fta/EMFTAGenerator.java

PART 3: SYSTEM ANALYSIS WITH AADL

As with all other analysis tools, the first thing to do is create the system instance for your model using the following steps:

1. In the OSATE outline, right-click the system implementation that is your root system.
2. Select the Instantiate System option as shown below.

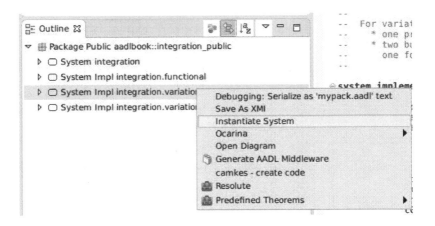

Instantiate the system implementation first

The FTA analysis runs against the system instance, which is located in the `instances/` directory in the Explorer view. To invoke the analysis, follow these steps as shown in the figure below:

1. Select the instance file.
2. Click on the Analyses menu.
3. Select the Fault Analyses option.
4. Select the Export to EMFTA option.

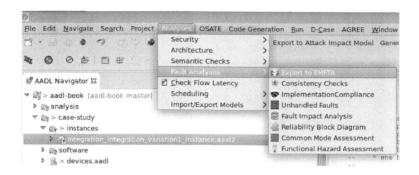

Select the system instance and invoke the analysis tool (Export to EMFTA)

When you invoke the plug-in, it will check that the root system of your instance model has an attached error model annex subclause with a `composite error model`. If that subclause is missing, the plug-in will display a dialog error to report the error. Otherwise, it will show a dialog box that invites the passenger to select the `error state` under analysis, as shown below. The analysis `error state` will then produce a fault tree whose root event is the selected `error state`.

Fault-Tree Analysis

(i) Select the Failure Mode to Analyze (error state, propagation) for 'integration_functional_Instance'

Error-Mode   state FailStop ▼

☐ Full tree

(?)   Cancel   OK

PART 3: SYSTEM ANALYSIS WITH AADL

Select the error state in the Error-Mode dropbox

Once the error state is selected, the fault tree is generated and opened in the embedded Eclipse FTA editor, as shown below. There is no need to open the diagram with an external editor; the error model tools already include an FTA visualizer and editor. For our case study, the generated FTA is huge: As shown in the following picture, it is definitely too big to be read in a book. The advantage is that by using a model, we can automate the production of the FTA and avoid doing it by hand!

The FTA for our case study
(probably too big for a book format!)

Fault Impact

Fault impact analysis shows the impact of each error source within the system. In terms of AADL, the analysis reports each error flow and shows each flow element (`error source`, `error path`, and `error sink`). Also, it reports any error event that propagates errors to other components. In this case, the `error event` has to trigger a state change when the component propagates a specific error. For example, in our case study, the `speed_controller` process switches to the `FailStop` state when receiving the `Failure error event` and then propagates the `ItemOmission` error type on the `speed_cmd` and brake_cmd features while in this state. The Failure error event will then be considered as the beginning of a flow reported by the analysis tool. An extract of the EBSM of this component is shown below.

```
component error behavior
transitions
    t0 : Operational -[Failure]-> FailStop;
propagations
    p0 : FailStop -[]-> speed_cmd{ItemOmission};
    p1 : FailStop -[]-> brake_cmd{ItemOmission};
end component;
```

Component error behavior of the speed controller

If a single error source or error event is connected to multiple flows and ultimately reaches several error sinks, the fault impact analysis will report each of them. In other words, to use the fault impact analysis on your AADL model, you need to declare error flows with error source, error path, and error sink elements. The tool will then retrieve the flows and report them in the CSV[67] format that you can read using a spreadsheet tool such as LibreOffice.[68]

---

[67] https://en.wikipedia.org/wiki/Comma-separated_values
[68] http://libreoffice.org/

PART 3: SYSTEM ANALYSIS WITH AADL

How Can You Use the Analysis?

As for all other analyses, the AADL model under analysis needs to be instantiated. To instantiate your system instance, in the OSATE outline, using these steps:

1. Right-click the system implementation of your root system.
2. Select the Instantiate System option as shown below.

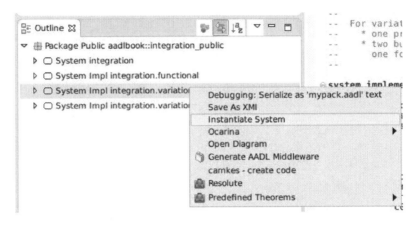

Instantiate the system implementation first

The FTA analysis runs against the system instance, which is located in the `instances/` directory in the Explorer view of Eclipse. To invoke the analysis, follow these steps as shown in the figure below:

1. Select the instance file.
2. Click the Analyses menu.
3. Select the Fault Analyses option.
4. Select the Fault Impact Analysis option.

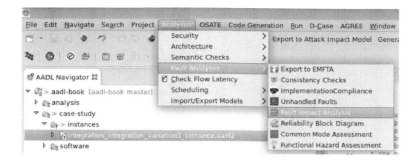

Select the system instance and invoke the analysis tool

The tool stores the name of the analyzed system instance in a new CSV file located in the `reports/FaultImpact` directory. You can open the file with any productivity tool. If you have trouble doing that, right-click the filename and select the Open With option and then the System editor option, or choose the Other option to open the file with a different program.

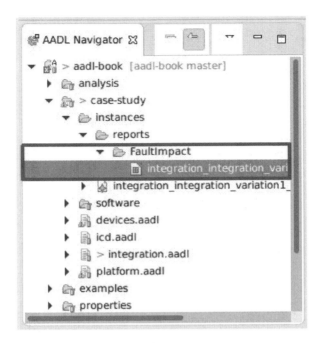

**The location of the generated Fault Impact report
(shown in the Explorer view of OSATE)**

For each error flow in the generated report, there is one line that starts with an `error source` and ends with an `error sink`. In between, all the `error paths` of the error flow are listed. The following picture shows an extract of the analysis results for our case study. For each flow, the report indicates the component and its initial failure mode and then the effect at each flow element (i.e., how the error is propagated through the architecture and finally reaches other components).

To illustrate this, we will inspect the last error flow of the report (from `panel` to `screen`). In this error flow, the initial error is raised from the `panel` component. This component emits the `ItemOmission` error on its `increase_speed` interface and propagates it to the `panel_controller` component, on its `increase_speed` interface. The `panel_controller` receives the `ItemOmission` error and propagates it to the screen component on the `desired_speed` interface. It then impacts the screen component, and the propagation stops there.

Component	Initial Failure Mode	1st Level Effect	Failure Mode	Second Level Effect	Failure Mode
speed_voter	internal event Failure	{AboveRange} speed -> speed_ctrl.current_speed	speed_ctrl {AboveRange}	{OutOfRange} speed_cmd -> acceleration.cmd	acceleration {OutOfRange} {Masked}
speed_voter	internal event Failure	{AboveRange} speed -> speed_ctrl.current_speed	speed_ctrl {AboveRange}	{ItemOmission} warning -> screen.warning	screen {ItemOmission} {Masked}
speed_ctrl	internal event Failure	{AboveRange} brake_cmd -> brake.cmd	brake {AboveRange} {Masked}		
panel	{ItemOmission}	{ItemOmission} increase_speed -> panel_controller.increase_speed	panel_controller {ItemOmission}	{OutOfRange} desired_speed -> screen.desired_speed	screen {OutOfRange} {Masked}
panel	{ItemOmission}	{ItemOmission} increase_speed -> panel_controller.increase_speed	panel_controller {ItemOmission}	{OutOfRange} desired_speed -> screen.desired_speed	screen {OutOfRange} {Masked}

The generated Fault Impact report in LibreOffice

Using a CSV file for the fault impact analysis provides an opportunity to easily compare several variations of the same architecture (by comparing the values within the CSV file or just the number of lines). As typical safety-critical systems have fault impact analysis that involves thousands of error flows, automating such reports facilitates certification efforts.

Summary of Modeling Artifacts Per Analysis

The following table lists all modeling elements used for each analysis. The objective is twofold: have a small cheat sheet for AADL users but also show how a model-based approach can simplify system analysis while making results more consistent. First, as the same information is used across analyses, a model-based approach avoids the need to enter information twice, as with typical, manual analyses. Second, as all analyses automatically reuse the same information, all information from generated documents will be consistent, avoiding potential human errors that occur with manually produced documents.

Analysis Method	Relevant EMV2 elements
Functional Hazard Assessment	• `error source` • `error events` • `emv2::occurrencedistribution` property • `emv2::severity` property • `emv2::likelihood` property • `emv2::hazards` property
Fault Tree Analysis	• Error flows: `error source`, `error path` and `error sink` • `error behavior state machine` • `error events` • `composite error behavior` • `emv2::occurrencedistribution` property
Failure Mode and Effects Analysis	• Error flows: `error source`, `error path` and `error sink` • `error behavior state machine` • `error events`

Summary of modeling elements used for each analysis

Questions

1. Why do analysis tools use a system instance rather than a component declaration to perform the analysis?
2. Which AADL architecture elements impact system latency?
3. Why is an AADL annex necessary for fault modeling?
4. Can you identify the main difference between fault impact analysis and Fault Tree Analysis?

Part 4: Extending AADL

Available Extension Mechanisms

There are two ways to augment an AADL model and add characteristics other than those defined in the core language: **user-defined properties** and **annexes**.

User-defined AADL properties enable you to augment the set of properties available in the language, and using them is a quick and simple way to add new characteristics to the AADL elements (e.g., components, features, connections). They do not need specific tool support: The built-in AADL parser included in any good tool will parse the property and make it available for the user.

AADL annexes are more complex: They augment the core language with new elements, but, because they need a specific parser, they are not supported natively by the existing compiler. You must support (and maintain) your own annex language yourself, which is a lot of work.

Before starting your own language extension, you should carefully consider both options.

Which Is the Best Mechanism for You?

There is no definitive, quick answer to this. If you want to add a characteristic of your model, such as a configuration directive for one element, the property mechanism is probably the best mechanism: It will only take a few minutes to define a new property set and write the property definition you want. But if your objective is to augment the architecture description with new features, you might need to associate a new language. Depending on the complexity of the annex language and what you want to do with it, it can take from a few hours to a few months.

The table below summarizes the pros and cons of both extension methods.

	Pros	Cons
User-defined properties	• Quick and simple • Support through AADL parser • Tool support	• Expressivity (limited to what property applies to and add a single value)
Annexes	• Expressivity (can define your own language within AADL)	• Tool support • Learning curve for the user

Pros and cons of using user-defined properties and annexes

Example of an AADL Extension

Now, let's take a look at two extensions: the ARINC653 annex extension (written by the author of this book) and the Error Model Annex [AADL-EMV2].

The ARINC653 extension relies solely on new AADL properties. There is no need for a new language: The ARINC653 extension defines the different configuration directives for an ARINC653 system (e.g., partitions scheduling, communication across partitions) using properties, and these directives are more than enough. By limiting ourselves to new properties, we ensure that users can use the extensions in any decent AADL tool (any parser can then use the property set) and avoid any tedious implementation work. Writing the ARINC653 properties took me half a day (the most time-consuming activity was writing the related standardization document).

The Error Model Annex (EMV2) doesn't just define configuration directives and static characteristic properties of the system: It also augments the architecture description with error flows, state machines, error propagations, relationships between incoming and outgoing faults, etc. The property mechanism was definitely not enough to support our model, which is why we implement it through a new annex language (EMV2). Since we wanted to support the language and use it for analysis purposes (generating FTA, fault impact, etc.), it took us some time to write a parser and the necessary tool support for it. After six months, we had an initial prototype with some analysis capabilities. Even now, OSATE developers are still improving the code and of course, addressing bug reports from users. This new expressivity comes at a price, and it is better to know what you need and how you are going to implement it before wasting your time!

AADL Properties

Introducing new AADL properties is the easiest way to extend the language. The AADL core language already defines common ones used in many safety-critical or real-time systems (referred to as standard properties), but you can define your own custom properties if you like.

PART 4: EXTENDING AADL

Benefits of Properties

In addition to being easy to add, properties offer free benefits to the modeler such as built-in type checking. Properties are types that are strongly typed so that the AADL parser automatically checks the correctness of property declarations. Also, the property type mechanism uses units, which avoid some typical mistakes such as type unit mismatch. For example, if you have a property weight without any unit, your model analysis tool makes an assumption about the unit being used. This is an implicit agreement between the analysis tool (that will assume one unit for doing the calculation) and the modeler (that has to make sure all values are using the same units). By defining the unit and specifying the relation between them, this knowledge becomes explicit in the model: The modeler must explicitly specify the unit, and the analysis tool can convert between different units.

Now, let's look at an example! Note that this example is on my GitHub repository at https://github.com/juli1/aadl-book/tree/master/eclipse-project/properties.[69] There, you'll find the `use-myproperties.aadl` file that uses two properties to define weights:

- `weight`: defines a property to specify the weight of a component using different units. We define the unit relation and how to convert from one unit to the other: The `weight_units` property specifies that a kilogram (kg) is 100 grams (g) and a pound is 453.59 grams.

---

[69]   https://github.com/juli1/aadl-book/tree/master/eclipse-project/properties

PART 4: EXTENDING AADL

- badweight: defines a property for specifying the weight without units

The following AADL listing shows the definition of the units as well as the two properties.

```
property set myproperties is
    weight_units: type units
        (g, kg => g * 1000,
        pound => g * 453.59,
        ton => kg * 1000);
    weight : aadlreal units
            myproperties::weight_units
applies to (system, device, processor, memory);

    badweight : aadlreal
applies to (system, device, processor, memory);
end myproperties;
```

AADL listing of unit and property definitions

Next, let's review the difference between weight and badweight and how they impact the analysis using a simple system composed of a sensor that weighs 1.0 pound and a sensor that weighs 100 grams.

In our first implementation, which uses the badweight property, we just report the weight without units. When computing the weight of the global system, the best thing an analysis tool can do is simply to add the weight of the subcomponents and report that the weight is 101, without any unit. In this case, the tool assumes all weights are defined with the same unit.

```
system implementation integration.without_units
subcomponents
```

```
    m : device motor;
    s : device sensor;
properties
    myproperties::badweight => 100.0
                applies to s;
    myproperties::badweight => 1.0
                applies to m;
end integration.without_units;
```

Using the `badweight` property

Our second implementation uses the unit system, which associates the value of 100 grams to the sensor and 1.0 pound to the motor. Using the units definition, the analysis tool computes the total weight for a specific unit. In that case, the total weight of the system implementation will be 454.59 grams. The AADL compiler does the conversion automatically for you and avoids the error-prone manual conversion. This is an additional AADL safety net that's pretty simple, but conversion errors happen often when designing safety-critical systems, especially when using components from different teams/countries.

```
system implementation integration.with_units
subcomponents
    m : device motor;
    s : device sensor;
properties
    myproperties::weight => 100.0 g
            applies to s;
    myproperties::weight => 1.0 pound
            applies to m;
end integration.with_units;
```

System implementation with weight using different units

PART 4: EXTENDING AADL

Another benefit of using properties is the sanity check you get regarding where the property is defined. The property definition specifies which AADL element it can be applied to. If the modeler is trying to assign the property to an element whose category is not authorized in the property definition, the compiler will raise an issue, and the model will be tagged as invalid. This free feature ensures that properties are defined consistently in the model.

Defining a New Property

Like models, user-defined properties are defined in files using the AADL extension. However, AADL properties are defined in a property set that contains multiple properties, each with a type and an optional unit. The standard specifies the following predefined types you can reuse in your property set:

- `aadlinteger`: an integer/number
- `aadlboolean`: Like any Boolean in programming language, this takes the true/false value.
- `aadlreal`: a real/float value (must have the decimal value defined)
- `enumeration`: Similar to an enumeration in C, this is a list of potential values. The AADL compiler will check for the use of appropriate values.
- `record`: Similar to a structure in C, this has several members with a particular type.

A property can be single- or multi-valued (using a list) and, if desired, a default value. For example, if you define a property for component weight with a default value of 0, components that don't explicitly define this property will have an automatically assigned value of 0.

PART 4: EXTENDING AADL

To see how to define properties, let's look at an example with a property set. For example, I want to add the following properties in a property set called `newproperties`:

- description: describes each AADL system component. This property is a single string, and its default is set to "description empty."
- reviews: contains comments from a reviewer about any model element
- weight: specifies the weight of a system, device, processor, or memory. The weight is characterized with a real number and has a unit.

We declare the description property as a string that can be attached to each system component and ensure that we filter the component type correctly in the `applies to` clause of the property definition.

```
description : aadlstring =>
     "unknown description" applies to (system);
```

The `description` property definition

The `reviews` property is more difficult and requires the use of a new type that defines a record. The record has three parts:

- author: a string that identifies an author
- importance: an enumeration that indicates if the review is major or minor
- content: the content of the review (i.e., the reviewer's comments)

Once this type is defined, we can define the property that specifies the list of reviews. It is simply a list of review types that can be applied to all AADL elements (components, features, connections, etc.). When a property applies to all elements, the `all` keyword is used in the `applies to` clause . Here's the declaration of the new type and the associated `reviews` property:

```
review_type       : type record (
   author         : aadlstring;
   importance     : enumeration (major, minor);
   content        : aadlstring;
);
reviews : list of myproperties::review_type
                          applies to (all);
```

The `reviews` property definition

The definition of the `weight` property is more interesting because it involves a units definition. Before defining the property, we define a new unit, `weight_units`. We define the relation between each unit (e.g., how much a pound is in grams). Our new `weight_units` type defines the following units: gram, kilogram, and pound. The unit definition explicitly defines how to convert one unit into another, e.g., from a pound to a gram. Here's this new unit's definition:

```
weight_units: type units
   (g,  kg => g * 1000,
    pound => g * 453.59,
    ton => kg * 1000);
```

The `weight_units` definition

Once the type is defined, we can define the new property that will use it. The property is a real number (`aadlreal`) that takes the unit defined previously. The properties apply only to hardware (physical) components, such as devices, processors, memory, or systems. Here is the definition of the property:

```
weight : aadlreal units
myproperties::weight_units
applies to (system, device, processor, memory);
```

The weight property definition

Using a New Property

Using the property requires two steps:
1. Include the package that declares the property in the with clause.
2. Define the property in the component or its parent.

Adding the package in the with clause is simple: Just add the property set name. In the case of our new property set, we include the following statement:

```
with myproperties
```

The with clause

Next, we declare the property value either in the component or its parent.

Declaring a property in the component: The property value is declared in the property section of the component (either the type or implementation). For example, if you have a component motor and want to declare the property weight and reviews, you would use this code:

```
device motor
properties
  myproperties::reviews =>
  (
  [author => "Bob";
   importance => minor;
   content => "This component needs feature!";
  ],
  [author => "Jack";
   importance => major;
   content => "Needs to describe the behavior";
  ]
  );
  myproperties::weight => 1.0 pound;
end motor;
```

Declaring properties for the motor component

About property names
The property name **is always** prefixed with the property set name unless it's a standard property. This avoids any confusion between property sets using the same property name.

Declaring a property in the parent: The property is declared in a component's parent, not in the component itself. This way of defining properties is convenient when the property value depends on other factors that are decided during instantiation. When declaring a property this way, you use an additional applies to clause at the end of the property value that specifies which component (the path to the AADL elements) the property applies to. The following example shows how to define the property weight on the s sensor contained in a system implementation:

159

```
system implementation integration.i
subcomponents
    m : device motor;
    s : device sensor;
properties
    myproperties::weight => 100.0 g
                                applies to s;
end integration.i;
```

**Defining a property on the s sensor
in the component's parent**

Examining Property Values in a Model

OSATE includes a graphical property values editor that provides a convenient way to view and define property values for a given component and see the defaults set in the core language. This editor works in the declarative and instance AADL model. When the editor is in a component (declarative model) or selecting an instance element (instance model), the property values editor shows the actual property value. The next section explains how to open this editor.

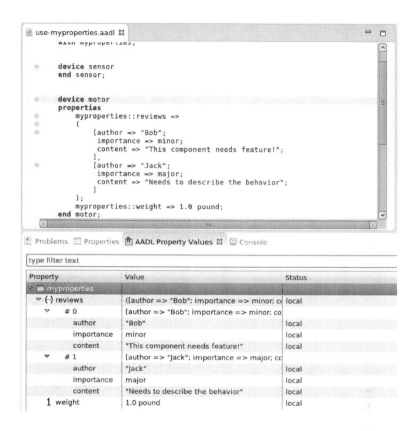

Viewing properties of a component in the property values editor

PART 4: EXTENDING AADL

Using the Property Editor in OSATE

To graphically use the AADL Property Values editor, make sure you're in the AADL perspective (the AADL logo should appear in the upper right-hand corner of the window, as highlighted by the green box in the picture below). Then, follow these steps:

1. Click on the Window menu.
2. Select the Show View option.
3. Select the AADL Property Values option.

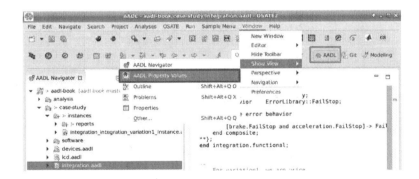

Selecting the AADL Property Values option

Then, you'll see the following window in your Eclipse environment, often collocated close to the Eclipse Properties and the Problem views. This view shows all the AADL properties for a given element, either in the instance or declarative model. Four buttons are available, highlighted with the red, yellow, green, and blue boxes:

- **Collapse all** (red box): collapses all the views

- **Show all/show imported properties** (yellow box): shows either all properties (including those defined by default) or only imported properties (those imported using a `with` statement)
- **Show undefined properties** (green box): shows all properties, even the ones not defined. It basically shows all properties available in the modeling framework.
- **Show default property values** (blue box): shows properties that are defined by default (in the property declaration)

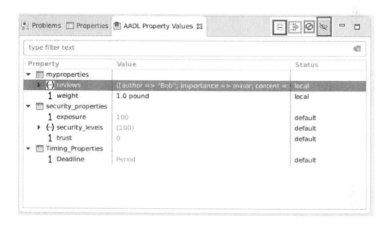

Opening the AADL Property Values view

Looking at Existing Property Definitions

It might definitively help you to look at actual property definitions if you plan to design your own properties. Looking at how the standard properties are defined will help you to define your own!

All properties that are embedded in any AADL plug-in are stored in the OSATE environment in the AADL Navigator, under `Plugin_Resources`. The following picture shows the organization of the `Plugin_Resources` directory. The `Predeclared_Property_Sets` directory contains all the properties from the AADL standard. You don't need to include these properties in your model using a `with` clause in order to use them. The other properties are not in the standard and have been added by another plug-in.

- ▼ 📘 Plugin_Resources
  - ▶ 📂 aadl2rtos_resource
  - ▼ 📂 Predeclared_Property_Sets
    - ▶ 📄 AADL_Project.aadl
    - ▶ 📄 Communication_Properties.aadl
    - ▶ 📄 Deployment_Properties.aadl
    - ▶ 📄 Memory_Properties.aadl
    - ▶ 📄 Modeling_Properties.aadl
    - ▶ 📄 Programming_Properties.aadl
    - ▶ 📄 Thread_Properties.aadl
    - ▶ 📄 Timing_Properties.aadl
  - ▶ 📄 ARINC429.aadl
  - ▶ 📄 ARINC653.aadl
  - ▶ 📄 ARP4761.aadl
  - ▶ 📄 Base_Types.aadl
  - ▶ 📄 behavior_properties.aadl
  - ▶ 📄 Cheddar_Properties.aadl
  - ▶ 📄 Data_Model.aadl
  - ▶ 📄 deployment.aadl
  - ▶ 📄 EMV2.aadl
  - ▶ 📄 ErrorLibrary.aadl
  - ▶ 📄 MILSTD882.aadl
  - ▶ 📄 pok_properties.aadl
  - 📄 representations.aird (Modified)
  - ▶ 📄 Resolute_Stdlib.aadl
  - ▶ 📄 security_properties.aadl
  - ▶ 📄 security_theorems.aadl
  - ▶ 📄 SEI.aadl

The Plugin_Resources hierarchy

PART 4: EXTENDING AADL

AADL Annexes

AADL annexes are more complex than properties: While properties give you the ability to annotate AADL elements with some values, AADL annexes allow you to bind another language to a component. This is an "annex" to the component—something that is not defined in the language but augments the component's specification.

This additional information about the component is very useful from a specification perspective (so that the description is more accurate) but also from an analysis perspective: Analysis tools can use this additional language to improve analysis results.

AADL annex clauses are added at the end of the component, as shown below. They use the `annex` keyword, followed by the annex name and then everything between `{**` and `**}` is the annex content.

```
system mycomponent
annex annex_name {**
   -- content of the annex
   -- defined by the annex language
**};
end mycomponent;
```

Example of annex clause

The designer of the annex is free to choose any name for annex_name. For example, the EMV2 uses the name EMV2 [AADL-EMV2], while the Behavior Annex [AADL-BA] uses the name behavior_annex. This identifier is used by the AADL parser to call another parser that will be able to analyze the annex language.

PART 4: EXTENDING AADL

The case study already uses the EMV2, which augments the component description and provides information about safety and error management.

```
device camera
features
  picture : out data port
                aadlbook::icd::picture;
annex EMV2 {**
  use types          ErrorLibrary;

  error propagations
   picture : out propagation {ItemOmission};
  end propagations;
**};
end camera;
```

Use of the Error Model Annex v2 on the camera component

Benefits of the Annex Extension Mechanism

The first benefit is the freedom we give to the user: You are not constrained by the AADL language itself, so you can annotate the model with the language you want. You can also associate your own language with some AADL elements, as in the EMV2 or Behavior Annex.

On the other hand, developing your own annex language takes a lot of effort. If you want your annex to be parsed in Eclipse, you need to implement all the support for your annex: parser, analyzer, user interface elements, etc. This is a very work-intensive task, so before starting your own annex, you should seriously consider if you can just use the property mechanism instead.

PART 4: EXTENDING AADL

How to Implement an Annex

There are two distinct parts to designing an AADL annex: the language design part, which is totally tool-independent, and an implementation part, which creates all the software to support the annex in a modeling framework.

For the first part, you're on your own: You can write the annex specification in a text file using your favorite text editor. It's a good idea to discuss your design on the AADL mailing lists[70] so that people can also tell you if it has been already created in other projects. In addition, you should look at the EMV2 [AADL-EMV2] and Behavior Annex [AADL-BA], which have been standardized by the AADL committee.

For the second part, implementing the annex depends on your modeling tool: OSATE, Ocarina, AADL inspector, MASIW, etc. Each tool has a different way of implementing annex mechanisms. For OSATE, there's a tutorial that guides you through the implementation of an annex sub-language on the AADL wiki.[71] In a nutshell, the main steps to implementing a language annex are: creating a plug-in, defining the BNF (Backus-Naur Form) of the language, generating the parser, writing an analyzer, and interfacing with the AADL parser. This is a very long process, and supporting a new annex language can takes days to months, depending on your coding abilities.

---

[70] https://wiki.sei.cmu.edu/aadl/index.php/Mailing_List
[71] http://www.aadl.info/

Annex Examples

Several AADL annexes are already integrated into OSATE, including the Error Model Annex v2 [AADL-EMV2], the Behavior Annex [AADL-BA], Resolute [RESOLUTE] (an AADL-dedicated constraint language), and AGREE [AGREE].

The source code for EMV2 and the Behavior Annex is available on the OSATE GitHub repository.[72] RESOLUTE and AGREE are available on the GitHub code repository from SMACCM.[73] If you're considering designing and implementing an annex language, I strongly recommend looking at the source code to see how the language is implemented and integrated with the OSATE code base.

Designing an OSATE Plug-In

Once you design your model, you might want to make a new tool to analyze your system. OSATE already includes several analysis plug-ins to analyze different characteristics (e.g., weight, latency, safety), and you might want to modify them or just design your own plug-in. This section explains how to get started and write your first analysis plug-in.

Note: This section is OSATE-specific.

This section is specific to OSATE,[74] the Eclipse-based modeling framework for AADL. After reading this section,

---

[72]   https://github.com/osate/
[73]   https://github.com/smaccm/smaccm/
[74]   http://osate.org

you should know the basics of designing an AADL analysis plug-in. However, keep in mind that this solution is specific to OSATE and its implementation of AADL. If you want to design a plug-in for another platform, you'll have to learn the internal mechanisms of that platform and how it's implemented the AADL language.

About OSATE Internals

OSATE was the first AADL modeling environment. The first version of OSATE that supports AADL v1 was prototyped by CMU-SEI researchers, during their free time. When AADL received more attention, more people joined the development team, and OSATE started to be a real product.

The AADL meta-model is designed with the Eclipse Modeling Framework (EMF).[75] EMF lets you design your meta-model using the Ecore notation. From this notation, EMF has tools for generating Java classes that match your meta-model description. For example, in the AADL meta-model, there is a class for each component type: a Process class, a System class, and so on. You can see all the classes in the org.osate.aadl2[76] project in the OSATE sources.[77] Generated classes from the Ecore meta-model have getters and setters methods. So, if you want to get a subcomponent, a property, or anything else, you can just try to look at methods with the `get` prefix.

---

[75]   http://www.eclipse.org/modeling/emf/

[76]   https://github.com/osate/osate2-core/tree/develop/org.osate.aadl2

[77]   https://github.com/osate/osate2-core

PART 4: EXTENDING AADL

When switching from OSATE 1 to OSATE 2, there was a transition period where we started to change the way to parse AADL. In fact, we started to use Xtext,[78] a framework that lets you design your own domain-specific language and integrate it into Eclipse. In fact, we use Xtext for parsing, analyzing, and associating textual elements with EMF objects.

Set Up Your Development Environment

In order to develop anything for AADL, you need to set up your development environment, which involves installing a new Eclipse distribution, checking out OSATE sources, and installing dependencies (libraries, etc.). Hopefully, there's a tutorial available on the OSATE wiki[79] that guides you through all the steps to set up your development environment. I highly recommend you follow these detailed instructions available on the OSATE wiki[80] or at osate.org:[81]

1. Make sure you have Java 8 installed on your computer.
2. Download a fresh version of Eclipse.
3. Install all dependencies (you can install them all at once using a p2f file in Eclipse).
4. Check out the OSATE sources (look for a Team Project Set in the tutorial).

Once you've done that, the sources should build correctly, and you should be all set to start a new plug-in!

---

[78] http://www.eclipse.org/Xtext/
[79] https://wiki.sei.cmu.edu/aadl/index.php/Getting_Osate_2_sources
[80] http://www.aadl.info/
[81] http://www.osate.org/

PART 4: EXTENDING AADL

Set Up an Initial Eclipse Plug-In

An OSATE plug-in is, in fact, a simple Eclipse plug-in that lives in the Eclipse workspace and uses the Eclipse extension mechanisms to add more capabilities. We use it to add new parsers, menu entries, perspectives, etc.

To start a new Eclipse plug-in project:
1. Click the File menu.
2. Select the New and Others option.
3. Select the Plug-In Project option.
4. In the name section, type `mypluginproject`.
5. Continue until the wizard asks for a template. Then, select the Hello, World Command template as shown below.

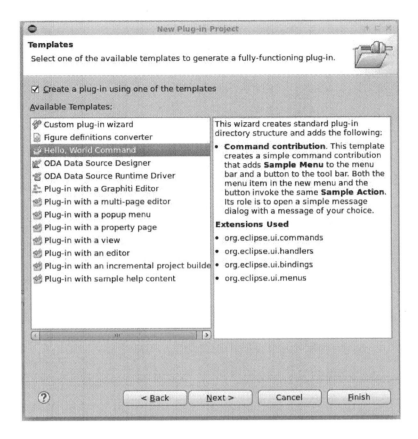

Select the Hello, World template

You can see the structure of the plug-in file below. This is a brief summary of the role of each file or directory:

- `src/`: contains the source of your plug-in
- `plugin.xml`: contains information on Eclipse extensions—new menus, help files, and everything else that extends the Eclipse platform. You must edit this file in order to add a menu entry to the Eclipse platform or a new file to the `Plugin_Resources` directory of the AADL perspective.

- META-INF/: contains the MANIFEST.MF file, which includes build-packaging information (package name/version, dependencies, etc.)
- build.properties: information to build the plug-in, either for source or binary release

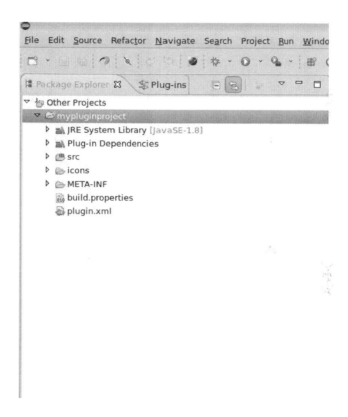

Eclipse explorer with the new plug-in

Starting the Hello, World Example

We now have a base Eclipse plug-in, so we need to try it and see how it works. To start it, we need to launch a new Eclipse instance that has the plug-in installed in it. To do that, follow these steps:

1. Click on the arrow to the right of the Debug button (as shown below in a red box).
2. Select the Debug Configuration option.

The debug icon: Click on the arrow to the right to show the contextual menu and create a new configuration

3. In the new window, select the Eclipse Application entry on the left.

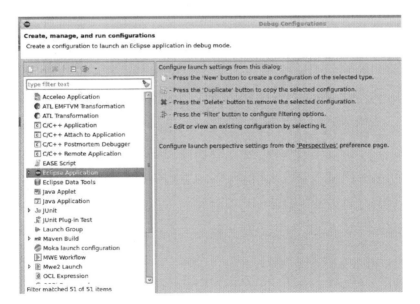

PART 4: EXTENDING AADL

Run configuration options

4. Next, follow these steps:
    a. In the Name field, specify the name of the new configuration (in the example screen below, I use plugintest).
    b. In the Program to Run section of the Main tab, click the Run a Project radio button and then specify the value
        `org.osate.branding.org.osate.product.`
    c. Click the Debug button.

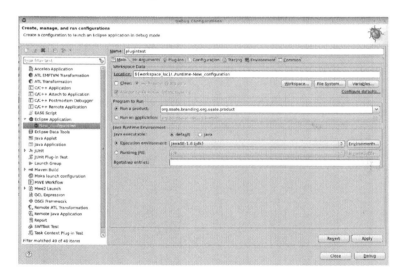

New debug configuration parameters

5. When the new OSATE instance starts and you see the Sample Menu, click on it.
6. Select the Sample Command option. When a window appears like the one shown below, you know that the

PART 4: EXTENDING AADL

Hello, World plug-in is working! The next section explains how to deal with AADL-specific aspects of this plug-in.

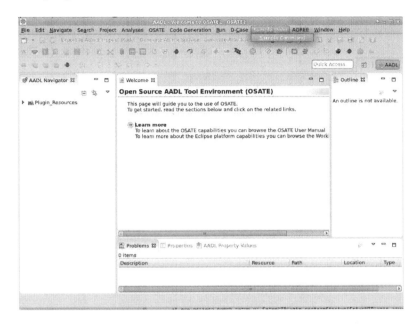

New sample command available

Result of the new command

PART 4: EXTENDING AADL

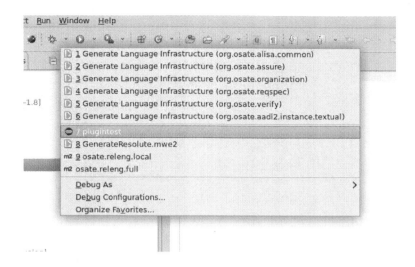

New debug configuration available directly

Dissecting the Hello, World Plug-In

So now, you might wonder how the Hello, World plug-in works, specifically how it adds a new menu item in Eclipse and how a new dialog appears when you select the menu.

First, look at the `plugin.xml` file at the root directory of your plug-in. In this file, these three main declarations are important:
- declaration of a new command
- association of the command with the handler
- declaration of a new menu option and associating a command with it

For each part, we declare an extension point that uses the `<extension>` XML tag. The first task is to declare a command. The important part is to make sure that the command has a unique identifier (attribute id).

```
<extension point="org.eclipse.ui.commands">
 <category name="Sample Category"
   id="mypluginproject.commands.category">
 </category>
 <command name="Sample Command"
 categoryId="mypluginproject.commands.category"
 id="mypluginproject.commands.sampleCommand">
 </command>
</extension>
```

Command declaration

Once the command is declared, we need to associate it with a handler. The handler is indicating how the command is implemented and more precisely, what Java class implements it. The referenced class must extend the AbstractHandler class. We present the SampleHandler class later. When declaring the handler, be sure to:

- Correctly specify the commandId element. It **must be** the same as the id elements in the command declared previously.
- Correctly specify the class with the full qualified name (including the package name).

```
<extension point="org.eclipse.ui.handlers">
   <handler    commandId=
       "mypluginproject.commands.sampleCommand"

class="mypluginproject.handlers.SampleHandler">
   </handler>
</extension>
```

Associating a command with a handler

PART 4: EXTENDING AADL

The last part declares a new menu option that will call the action defined earlier. In the following code example, we add a new option to the main menu (the type of menu is specified in the `locationURI` element). It's also possible to add menu entries to other elements of the platform.

In that specific case, we just declare a new menu called Sample Menu that contains the command referenced by the specified `id` element.

When declaring a new menu, be sure to specify:
* a unique ID for the menu item
* an existing command using the `id` attribute of the command element

```
<extension point="org.eclipse.ui.menus">
  <menuContribution
locationURI="menu:org.eclipse.ui.main.menu?afte
r=additions">
    <menu label="Sample Menu"
      id="mypluginproject.menus.sampleMenu">

    <command
commandId="mypluginproject.commands.sampleComma
nd"

      id="mypluginproject.menus.sampleCommand">
    </command>
  </menu>
  </menuContribution>
</extension>
```

Declaring new menu options

Now, it's time to show how the `SampleHandler` class works. This is very simple: The class must inherit the `AbstractHandler` class and define the `execute()`

method that's invoked when the handler is called. So, all the magic starts in this method!

In this plug-in, the class is just starting a dialog where the text "Hello, Eclipse world" is shown.

```
public class SampleHandler extends
AbstractHandler {
  public SampleHandler() {
  }

  public Object execute(ExecutionEvent event)
throws ExecutionException {
    IWorkbenchWindow window =
HandlerUtil.getActiveWorkbenchWindowChecked(eve
nt);
    MessageDialog.openInformation
        (window.getShell(), "Mypluginproject",
        "Hello, Eclipse world");
        return null;
  }
}
```

The SampleHandler class

Now, we need to learn how to read and process AADL elements so you can start your own AADL-specific plug-in. The next section details how to access AADL elements.

Adapting the Plug-In for AADL Analysis

For now, we have a plug-in that adds a menu to the Eclipse platform but does nothing AADL-related. In fact, this is a generic Eclipse plug-in. This section details how to add AADL-related code and all the necessary infrastructure to browse a model. We'll implement a simple plug-in that browses the model and counts the numbers of components, similar to the statistics plug-in available in OSATE. The full source code of the plug-in is available on the GitHub account related to this book.[82] Please check out the code if you want to build your own plug-in.

Now, we need to interact with the AADL model, which can basically read the AADL elements in the Java code. It will all start in the handler, which is the entry point of our plug-in. There, we'll do the following:

1. Get the element currently selected in the outline.
2. If this is a component implementation, instantiate it; if this is already a system instance, keep the selected element.
3. Print a message if we have a system instance.

The AADL `system Instance`, which represents the root of a system instance model, is mapped in Java with a `SystemInstance` object. Our goal will be to get this object from the component actually selected by the user.

The first step is to retrieve the selected object in the Eclipse framework. To do that, we get the current selection using the `HandlerUtil.getCurrentSelection()` method and then get the first item in that selection using the `getFirstElement()` method (on the selection object). This object should be an `EObject`, since it will be something that represents an AADL entity specified using the Eclipse Modeling Framework [EMF].

What is an EObject?

---

[82]   https://github.com/juli1/aadl-book

PART 4: EXTENDING AADL

An EObject is the lowest common denominator of all objects that are described using an Ecore meta-model. Eclipse includes the Eclipse Modeling Framework[83] [EMF], which gives the ability to specify a meta-model in a format called Ecore. Later, that meta-model description can be automatically generated into Java classes that will ultimately implement the meta-model. The classes will reflect the meta-model specification and map each object from the Ecore meta-model into a Java class. Each generated java class will inherit the EObject class without any exception. So, no matter what model you're using, each object that represents something from a meta-model will inherit the EObject class.

```
IStructuredSelection selection =
  (IStructuredSelection)
     HandlerUtil.getCurrentSelection(event);

IOutlineNode node =
     (IOutlineNode) selection.getFirstElement();

EObject selectedObject = (EObject) node;
```

Getting the selected EObject in OSATE

Now, we have the EObject that represents the AADL entity selected in the Outline view. But we don't know what type of AADL component it is. Is it a component instance or an already instantiated system implementation? We need to check that!

The first thing we do is check if the selectedObject variable is an instance of a SystemInstance. If it is, we have what we need! If it's a component implementation, it

---

83   https://en.wikipedia.org/wiki/Eclipse_Modeling_Framework

will be an instance of the `ComponentImplementation`
Java type. In that case, we'll instantiate the component
implementation that will create the new system instance.

```
if (selectedObject instanceof SystemInstance)
{
    rootInstance =
            (SystemInstance) selectedObject;
}


if (selectedObject instanceof
                    ComponentImplementation)
{
    try {
        rootInstance =
InstantiateModel.buildInstanceModelFile
    ((ComponentImplementation)selectedObject);

    } catch (Exception e) {
        e.printStackTrace();
    }
}
```

**Getting the selected object and automatically instantiate
component implementation**

If the selected component is neither a system instance nor a
component implementation, the code will not modify the
`rootInstance` variable: It will remain null. The plug-in
shows a dialog window indicating if a system
implementation has been found. After the code example
below, there's the dialog box opened by our program.

```
if (rootInstance == null)
```

```
{
   MessageDialog.openError
        (window.getShell(), "Error",
         "System instance not available");
}
else
{
   MessageDialog.openError
        (window.getShell(), "Error",
         "System instance has the name " +
         rootInstance.getName() );
}
```

Opening Dialog windows in OSATE

The following code shows the complete implementation of the updated execute() method of the SampleHandler class.

```
public Object execute(ExecutionEvent event)
throws ExecutionException {
   IWorkbenchWindow window =
HandlerUtil.getActiveWorkbenchWindowChecked
            (event);

   IStructuredSelection selection =
        (IStructuredSelection)
         HandlerUtil.getCurrentSelection(event);

   IOutlineNode node = (IOutlineNode)
               selection.getFirstElement();

   node.readOnly(new IUnitOfWork<Object,
EObject>() {
        public Object exec(EObject state) throws
Exception {
            SystemInstance rootInstance = null;
            EObject selectedObject = (EObject)
```

```
state;

        if (selectedObject instanceof
                            SystemInstance) {
            rootInstance =
                (SystemInstance) selectedObject;
        }
        if (selectedObject instanceof
            ComponentImplementation) {
            try {
                rootInstance =

InstantiateModel.buildInstanceModelFile

((ComponentImplementation)selectedObject);
            }
            catch (Exception e) {
                e.printStackTrace();
                return null;
            }
        }
        if (rootInstance == null) {
            MessageDialog.openError
             (window.getShell(),
        "Error", "System instance not available");
        }
        else
        {
            MessageDialog.openError
             (window.getShell(),
              "Information",
              "System instance has the name " +
              rootInstance.getName() );
        }
        return null;
    }
});
    return null;
}
```

The new handler code in SampleHandler.java

PART 4: EXTENDING AADL

When using this code, we started to use a lot of bundles, classes, and other libraries that aren't required by the simple Hello, World plug-in. Many more software components are required. To use these pieces of code, you need to declare them in a `META-INF/MANIFEST.MF` file such as the example one below that lists the dependencies, including those in the `Require-Bundle` and `Import-Package` sections. Before starting the plug-in, you must update the file and include all necessary packages/bundles. Otherwise, the AADL-related packages will not be loaded and therefore won't be available for your code.

```
Manifest-Version: 1.0
Bundle-ManifestVersion: 2
Bundle-Name: Mypluginproject
Bundle-SymbolicName:
mypluginproject;singleton:=true
Bundle-Version: 1.0.0.qualifier
Bundle-Activator: mypluginproject.Activator
Require-Bundle: org.eclipse.ui,
 org.eclipse.core.runtime,
 org.eclipse.core.resources;bundle-
version="3.10.1",
 org.osate.aadl2;bundle-version="1.0.0",
 org.osate.xtext.aadl2;bundle-version="1.0.0",
 org.osate.xtext.aadl2.properties;bundle-
version="1.0.0"
Bundle-RequiredExecutionEnvironment: JavaSE-1.8
Bundle-ActivationPolicy: lazy
Import-Package: org.eclipse.emf.ecore,
 org.eclipse.xtext.ui.editor.outline,
 org.osate.aadl2,
 org.osate.aadl2.instantiation
```

The updated MANIFEST.MF file

PART 4: EXTENDING AADL

Finally, we have to test the plug-in! To do that, follow these steps:

1. Start the Eclipse instance by clicking on the Debug icon.
2. Create a new AADL project.
3. Write a simple model that contains a system implementation.
4. Select the system instance object in the Outline view and invoke our plug-in. You should see a dialog box similar to the one shown below.

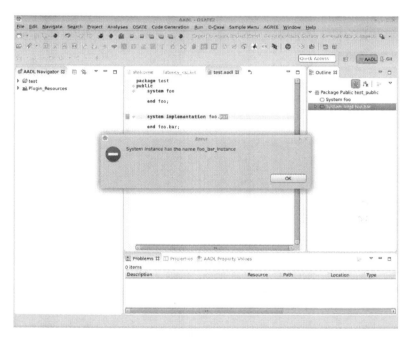

Example of plug-in execution with the system instance name

PART 4: EXTENDING AADL

Processing AADL Elements: A Simple Statistic Approach

We're now able to get an AADL element into the Java world and that gives us the ability to manipulate programmatically the components, connections, and properties of an AADL model. We will illustrate the manipulation of a model with a simple example: a piece of code that will produce some statistics about the model. The plug-in will report the number of components for each type.

In OSATE, a component instance is implemented with access methods and the `ComponentInstance` class, which contains interesting attributes. For example, the `getAllComponentInstances()` method returns a list of all subcomponent instances in the model, and the `getComponentInstances()` returns a list of all direct subcomponent instances. Similarly, `getFeatureInstances()` returns a list of all feature instances of the component.

For our simple statistics plug-in, we define a method that returns the number of components for a given component and component category (i.e., process, thread). We call this method `countNb()` and use the following arguments:

- `component`: the component instance to analyze, likely the root of the system instance
- `cat`: the component category to get. In OSATE, the `ComponentCategory` class enumerates all the different component categories of AADL. Each category is a specific `ComponentCategory` value.

We call the `getAllComponentInstances()` method that returns all the subcomponent instances of the current components and also call it recursively on all subcomponents. In other words, it returns all the component instances that are below the current component in the hierarchy. Basically, if you call this method on the root component of a model, the method will return the list of all subcomponents.

We leverage the Java 8 lambda mechanism to filter the list of all subcomponents and select only the ones with the category we're looking for (the `cat` argument for the function). The component category can be retrieved from an object using the `getCategory()` method.

```
public static int countNb
      (ComponentInstance component,
ComponentCategory cat)
{
   List<ComponentInstance> l =
     component.getAllComponentInstances()
   .stream()
      .filter (c -> c.getCategory() == cat)
        .collect(Collectors.toList());

   return l.size();
}
```

Function for counting the numbers of subcomponents of a given category

```
public Object execute(ExecutionEvent event)
throws ExecutionException {
   IWorkbenchWindow window =
HandlerUtil.getActiveWorkbenchWindowChecked(eve
nt);
   IStructuredSelection selection =
(IStructuredSelection)
```

```
        HandlerUtil.getCurrentSelection(event);

   IOutlineNode node = (IOutlineNode)
                 selection.getFirstElement();

   node.readOnly (new IUnitOfWork<Object,
EObject>() {
     public Object exec(EObject state) throws
Exception {
       SystemInstance rootInstance = null;
       EObject so = (EObject) state;

       if (so instanceof SystemInstance)
       {
         rootInstance = (SystemInstance) so;

       }

       if (so instanceof
ComponentImplementation) {
           try {
             rootInstance =
InstantiateModel.buildInstanceModelFile
           ((ComponentImplementation)so);

         }
         catch (Exception e) {
           e.printStackTrace();
           return null;
         }
       }
       StringBuilder sb = new StringBuilder();

       for (ComponentCategory cc :
             ComponentCategory.values())
       {
         sb.append("#" + cc + " - " +
           countNb(rootInstance, cc) + "\n");
       }

MessageDialog.openInformation
```

```
    (window.getShell(),
     "Component Statistics", sb.toString());
    return null;
    }
  }
);

  return null;
}
```

Updated Handler code

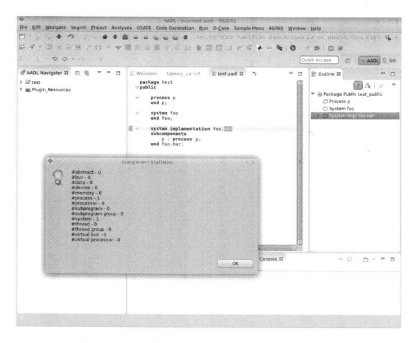

Example of the analysis plug-in result

PART 4: EXTENDING AADL

Second Plug-In: Generating Model Review Reports

Now, we'll design another plug-in that gathers all comments within a model and generates a report with all of them. The plug-in will use the `comments` property defined earlier in this chapter and store all the comments in a CSV file. The code source of the plug-in is available at GitHub.[84] To add it to your Eclipse environment, first import the Git repository[85] into your environment and then import the org.gunnm.aadl.commentreporting file.

This plug-in will add the AADL Reporting menu shown below for generating the report with all the comments.

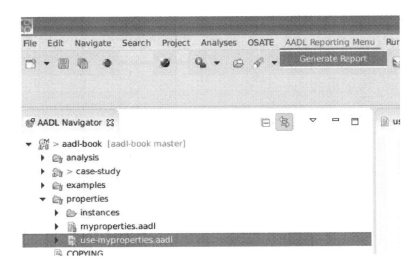

New menu item added by our plug-in

---

84   https://github.com/juli1/aadl-
      book/tree/master/org.gunnm.aadl.commentreporting
85   https://github.com/juli1/aadl-book.git

PART 4: EXTENDING AADL

Once you click on the AADL Reporting menu, a handler generates a report in a CSV file that contains all the comments for each component. The following pictures show the location of the report in the Eclipse explorer, as well as an example of the report for system implementation located in the `use-myproperties.aadl` file. You can find this file on our project on GitHub.[86]

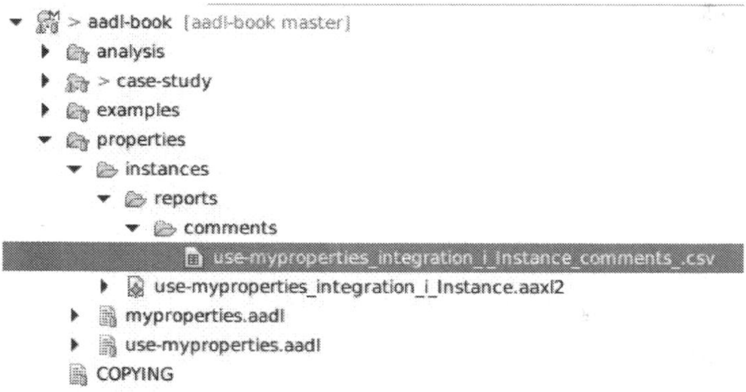

**Location of the file that contains
the new report (CSV file)**

---

86   https://github.com/juli1/aadl-book/blob/master/eclipse-project/properties/use-myproperties.aadl

Extract of the generated report with all comments information (author, content, importance) for each component

The objective is to guide you through the code and help you design similar analysis plug-ins that process properties. For that reason, we focus on the main code of the plug-in, especially the execute method of the Handler class, and don't discuss details discussed previously like how to add a specific menu.

First, we specify a Java class that represents a line entry on the report. Naturally, we call this class `Comment` and have an entry for each characteristic of a comment entry. The `name` member corresponds to the name of the component related to this comment.

```
class Comment {
    String author;    // author of the comment
    String content;   // content of the comment
    String importance;// importance
    String name;      // name of the component
```

```
    public Comment (String n, String a, String
c, String i)
    {
        name = n;
        author = a;
        content = c;
        importance = i;
    }
}
```

The Comment class

Next, we need a method that retrieves all comments for a given component, so we use the following `getComments()` command. The parameter is a `NamedElement`, a common object for AADL entities. The variable `ph` stands for Property Holder.

The first thing to do is resolve the property we want to use. The full qualified name of the property is `myproperties::reviews`. We look up the property using the following call:

```
property =
GetProperties.lookupPropertyDefinition(ph,
"myproperties", "reviews");
```

Lookup the myproperties::review property definition

If the property is nonexistent, the call will raise an exception.

Once the property is retrieved, we must get the value of the property associated with the component (if there is any). The `myproperties::reviews` property is a list that we get using the following call:

```
List<? extends PropertyExpression>
propertyValues =
ph.getPropertyValueList(property);
```

Getting property values for a component

From now on, the `propertyValues` variable contains a list of objects with the value `PropertyExpression`. The `PropertyExpression` type is the common denominator to all potential property expressions: integer, string, record, etc. In fact, you need to cast a `PropertyExpression` to the type you expect. In our case, `myproperties::reviews` contains a list of records, so we will cast it to a `RecordValue` object.

```
RecordValue rv = (RecordValue) pe;
```

Getting a RecordValue from a PropertyExpression

A record contains several members. In the case of our property, there are three members: author, content, and importance. The value of each is retrieved through a call to `GetProperties.getRecordField`. The following line shows how to get the author member.

```
PropertyAssociation pa =
GetProperties.getRecordField(fields,
"author");
```

Retrieving a PropertyAssociation from a Property Record

The call returns a `PropertyAssociation` that needs to be casted into the appropriate type: `StringLiteral` (for a string), `EnumerationLiteral`, `IntegerLiteral`, and so on. Our records are made of `StringLiteral` and `EnumerationLiteral`. We then cast the `PropertyAssociation` object to its appropriate type and retrieve the value.

```
pa = GetProperties.getRecordField
          (fields, "author");
String author =
((StringLiteral)pa.getValue()).getValue();

pa = GetProperties.getRecordField
          (fields, "content");
String content =
((StringLiteral)pa.getValue()).getValue();

pa = GetProperties.getRecordField
         (fields, "importance");

EnumerationLiteral elImportance =
(EnumerationLiteral)
((NamedValue)pa.getValue()).getNamedValue();
String importance = elImportance.getName();
```

Extracting the members of a Property Record

Finally, after retrieving the content from the comments, we can instantiate a new `comment` object and add it to the results. The name of the component can be obtained from the `ph` object, with a call to `ph.getName()`. Below, we show the complete code for the `getComments()` method.

197

```
public static List<Comment> getComments
            (final NamedElement ph) {
  Property property;
  List<Comment> result;
  BasicPropertyAssociation pa;

  result = new ArrayList<Comment> ();
  property =
      GetProperties.lookupPropertyDefinition
            (ph, "myproperties", "reviews");


  List<? extends PropertyExpression>
      propertyValues =
            ph.getPropertyValueList(property);

  for (PropertyExpression pe : propertyValues)
  {
    RecordValue rv = (RecordValue) pe;
    EList<BasicPropertyAssociation> fields =
        rv.getOwnedFieldValues();
    pa = GetProperties.getRecordField
                (fields, "author");
    String author =
      ((StringLiteral)pa.getValue()).getValue();

    pa = GetProperties.getRecordField
        (fields, "content");
    String content =
      ((StringLiteral)pa.getValue()).getValue();

    pa = GetProperties.getRecordField
        (fields, "importance");
    EnumerationLiteral elImportance =
      (EnumerationLiteral)
    ((NamedValue)pa.getValue()).getNamedValue();
    String importance = elImportance.getName();

    result.add
        (new Comment
  (ph.getName(), author, content, importance));
```

```
   }
   return result;
}
```

The full getComments() code

Now, that we have the getComments() method, we can build the CSV report: For each component of the system instance, we get all the comments. For each comment, we add a line into the CSV file. The following code shows how to do that, assuming that a root system instance is in a variable called rootInstance. Then, we add all the text of the CSV file into a StringBuffer object.

```
StringBuffer output = new StringBuffer();

output.append
    ("Component, Author,Content,Importance\n");

for (ComponentInstance ci :
rootInstance.getAllComponentInstances())
{
 List<Comment> comments = getComments(ci);
 for (Comment comment : comments)
 {
    output.append (comment.name);
    output.append (",");
    output.append (comment.author);
    output.append (",");
    output.append (comment.content);
    output.append (",");
    output.append (comment.importance);
    output.append ("\n");
 }
}
writeReport(rootInstance, output);
```

Building a CSV file from all Comment objects

Now, it's time to write the report into a file! First, it's essential to know where we'll be writing the report. In the example code below, getReportPath() gets the report path for a specific EObject. The EObject will be the system instance used to generate the report, so the newly created file location will be relative to this object location. The code gets the URI of the object in the modeling framework (with a call to OsateResourceUtil.getOsatePath()), removes the last segment (the file), and specifies the directory to put it in (/reports/comments). Finally, it specifies the file extension csv so that your system can identify which programs can open the file.

```
protected IPath getReportPath(EObject root) {
    String filename = null;
    Resource res = root.eResource();
    URI uri = res.getURI();
    IPath path =
            OsateResourceUtil.getOsatePath(uri);

    path = path.removeFileExtension();
    filename =
        path.lastSegment() + "_comments_";

    path = path.removeLastSegments(1)
        .append("/reports/comments/" + filename);
    path = path.addFileExtension("csv");
    return path;
}
```

Method to get the path to produce a report relative to the selected EObject

Now, we have all the pieces needed to write our report! The writeReport () function takes the system instance (root of your model instance) and the `StringBuffer` containing the report and writes the report on the filesystem. It gets the report path using the method detailed before `getReportPath ()` and either creates the file if it does not exist (and makes sure the folder and subfolders exist using a call to `AadlUtil.makeSureFoldersExist ())` or replaces the file's contents (if the file already exists).

```java
public void writeReport
        (EObject root, StringBuffer content) {
 IPath path = getReportPath(root);

 if (path != null) {
  IFile file = ResourcesPlugin.getWorkspace().
                getRoot().getFile(path);

  if (file != null) {
    final InputStream input =
      new ByteArrayInputStream
            (content.toString().getBytes());
    try {
      if (file.exists()) {
        file.setContents
            (input, true, true, null);
      } else {
        AadlUtil.makeSureFoldersExist(path);
        file.create(input, true, null);
      }

    }
    catch (final CoreException e)
    {
        System.out.println
            ("Something terribly happened!");
        e.printStackTrace ();
    }
  }
 }
}
```

```
}
```

Method to write a report in a file

Now, you should have the necessary foundation for designing your own AADL plug-in and be able to use either the standard core properties or your own, freshly defined properties! The code is available on the GitHub project of this book,[87] and we encourage you to reuse it for your own purposes.

Next, let's review some tips for developing a new plug-in. After years of developing, maintaining, and reading OSATE plug-in code, we know some good tips you might like!

Plug-In Development Tips

The GetProperties class

The `org.osate.xtext.aadl2.properties.util` project contains the `GetProperties` class. In this class, you have almost all the code needed to access properties and their values for components. Look at the method of this class to see which properties you can access.

For example, let's say that you want to retrieve the data size of a data component in bytes and the component is in the `dataComponent` variable. You can get the data size by calling the `getSourceDataSizeInBytes()` method from `GetProperties`:

---

87   https://github.com/juli1/aadl-book/tree/master/org.gunnm.aadl.commentreporting

```
double dataSize =
GetProperties.getSourceDataSizeInBytes
(dataComponent);
```

Getting the data size programmatically

Similarly, you can retrieve most of the other properties using methods from `GetProperties`. If you don't see a method to get the property you want, I highly recommend looking at the code in this class and mimicking its method to adapt it to your own property.

Converting Values with Different Units

AADL provides the ability to define property values with specific units. For example, we can specify the size using different units. For a data component, you can declare either

```
Data_Size => 1 KByte;
```

or

```
Data_Size => 1000 Bytes;
```

In fact, it does not matter which unit you use because the `Size_Units` property specifies that 1 Kbyte equals 1000 Bytes, as shown below. (You might wonder why 1Kbyte is not equal to 1024 Bytes, but this has been already discussed several times by the standardization committee. Read the standard for more information or even ask about the rationale via the AADL mailing list.)

```
Size_Units: type units (bits,
                        Bytes => bits * 8,
                        KByte => Bytes * 1000,
```

```
         MByte => KByte * 1000,
         GByte => MByte * 1000,
         TByte => GByte * 1000);
```

Definition of the size units in AADL

Now, as a plug-in programmer, one question you might ask is how you can get the value of a property, regardless of the units used in the property value. In fact, the model can declare the size in Mbytes, but you want to have the data size of all components in bytes to have consistent values (i.e., values with the same units).

The `getScaledNumberValue` method can do all the heavy lifting for you. This method, which you can find in `PropertyUtils.aadl` of the `org.osate.xtext.aadl2.properties.util` package, takes the following arguments:
- the property holder (argument ph)
- the property definition (argument pd)
- the unit you're expecting

```
public static double
getScaledNumberValue(final NamedElement ph,
final Property pd, final UnitLiteral unit);
```

Signature of the getScaledNumberValue method

PART 4: EXTENDING AADL

So, if your model declares the following component:

```
data mydata
properties
   data_size => 1 KByte;
end mydata;
```

Defining data size on a data component

A call to getScaledNumberValue() on that data component with the UnitLiteral set to "Bytes" will return 1000 because the Size_Units property declares that 1Kbyte = 1000 Bytes.

```
ComponentInstance dataComponent;

// retrieve the data component instance

Property dataSize = lookupPropertyDefinition
     (ne,"Memory_Properties", "Data_Size");

UnitLiteral unit =
        findUnitLiteral(dataSize, "Bytes");

Double value = PropertyUtils
     .getScaledNumberValue
        (dataComponent, dataSize, unit, 0.0);

System.out.println
     ("The data size is: " + value);
```

Getting and scaling the data size of a component instance

Browsing the AADL Java Objects

The AADL meta-model is specified using Ecore, a format specific to the Eclipse Modeling Framework. You can find the

PART 4: EXTENDING AADL

Ecore meta-model of the declarative and instance models in the org.osate.aadl2[88] project, in the `model/` directory.

The Java code of the declarative model generated from the Ecore meta-model is provided in the `src/org/osate/aadl2` directory of this project, and the Java code of the instance model is provided in the `src/org/osate/aadl2/instance` directory. When you're looking for a particular method, object, or class, these two are the best places to start your search. When you search these directories using the Eclipse search function, you often find a lot of useful information.

Instantiating the Model Programmatically

Sometimes, you have your system implementation object from the declarative but you want to create a system instance from that component (in order to start an analysis plug-in). We did this in our plug-in example. In fact, the instantiation code resided in the `InstantiateModel` class of the `org.osate.aadl2.instantiation` project.

For example, let's say you have a system implementation in a variable called `systemImpl` and want to get the instantiated system. To do that, you could use the following code:

```
SystemImplementation systemImpl;
ComponentInstance rootInstance;
/* … retrieve the system, do whatever you need */
rootInstance =
InstantiateModel.buildInstanceModelFile(systemI
```

88   https://github.com/osate/osate2-core/tree/develop/org.osate.aadl2

```
mpl);
```

Building a System Instance from a System Implementation Object

This piece of code will actually create an instance file in the `instances/` directory, where your model resides, and return a `SystemInstance` object that's the root component of your model. This method can throw some exceptions (e.g., when it's not possible to create the instance file), so you might put the call to `buildInstanceModelFile()` in a try/catch block.

Using CTRL+Space

Every IDE provides some convenient functions to assist programmers. One really useful function in Eclipse is the CTRL+space shortcut. If you press the CTRL, +, and spacebar keys simultaneously when you're typing in code, you'll see the list of all acceptable character sequences, variables, methods, etc. for that code.

The following screenshot shows the contextual menu that appears when you trigger the CTRL+Space key sequence.

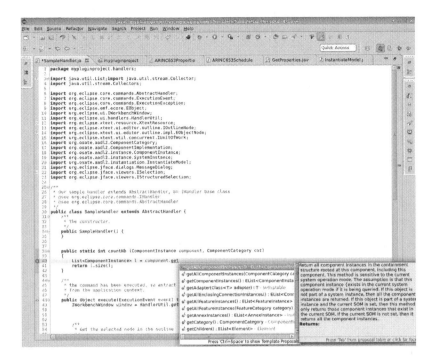

Contextual menu in Eclipse: the tool suggests all the methods that starts with the `get` suffix

Using Java 8 Lambda Expressions to Process a Model

Java 8 introduced the concept of lambda expressions. If you're not familiar with it, you can read about it online and even start on Wikipedia.[89] Lambda expressions can help write more readable and efficient code: Instead of writing tons of unreadable code for loops, you can efficiently write functions that will be applied on each element of a list.

---

[89]   https://en.wikipedia.org/wiki/Anonymous_function#Java

PART 4: EXTENDING AADL

The lambda expressions of Java 8 can be leveraged for writing AADL analysis plug-ins and are especially helpful when you're trying to iterate through the component/connection hierarchy. In fact, when using lambda expressions with AADL objects, you'll make an extensive use of `forEach()` and `filter()`.

The example from the plug-in shows how to use lambda expressions using `filter()`. In fact, when using the code below, we filter the list returned by `getAllComponentInstances()` using the function `c -> c.getCategory() == cat`.

```
List<ComponentInstance> l =
component.getAllComponentInstances()
    .stream()
      .filter (c -> c.getCategory() == cat)
         .collect(Collectors.toList());
```

Getting the component lists for a component using lambda functions

The same code is similar to the following version that's not using lambda expressions:

```
List<ComponentInstance> l =
        new ArrayList<ComponentInstance>();
for (ComponentInstance c :
        component.getAllComponentInstances())
{
    if (c.getCategory() == cat)
    {
      l.add(c);
    }
}
```

PART 4: EXTENDING AADL

Getting the component lists for a component without using lambda functions

You might notice that using the lambda expression makes the code more concise and easier to understand.

Next, let's review how we could use the `forEach()` construct. In the following code example, we use `forEach()` to print on the console the source and destination of each connection instance. The `rootInstance` variable is the root component of the AADL instance model.

```
rootInstance.getAllConnectionInstances()
    .forEach (conn->System.out.println
        ("source="+conn.getSource().getName() +
";destination="+conn.getDestination().getName()
));
```

Getting all connections instances using a lambda function

The same piece of code could be written without a lambda expression and would look like this:

```
for (ConnectionInstance conn :
rootInstance.getAllConnectionInstances())
{
    System.out.println
      ("source="+
        conn.getSource().getName() +
        ";destination="+
        conn.getDestination().getName());
}
```

Getting all connections instance without using a lambda function

Needless to say, using lambda expressions will save you time and make your code easier to maintain. I highly recommend using them. The only drawback is that it makes your code Java-8 specific, which is ultimately not a problem since OSATE requires Java 8.

Questions

1. What is OSATE? Eclipse? EMF? How do they relate to each other?
2. In which files of a plug-in project are Eclipse platform menus declared?
3. How can you get all the subcomponent instances of a particular component instance?
4. How can you get all the features of a particular component instance?
5. Can you write a method that takes a component instance in parameters and prints the component instance hierarchy on the standard output?
6. Can you write a method that prints the names of all component instances for which the classifier name is "foobar"?

Conclusion

Looking back at the history of computer science, we can see that designing good software is all about making the right level of abstractions and helping human developers express the system design and constraints with the right semantics to avoid ambiguity and bugs. Decades ago, this was done with programming languages that abstract the machine language and try to design one closer to natural language. Model-Based Engineering is the next abstraction level and tries to represent system concerns using an unambiguous, strong semantics. Tools process models to simulate, certify, or just implement the system with machine language. Believe it or not, this is where safety-critical software is headed. Products like SCADE are used for critical operations, and when you're flying, there's a fair chance that your plane runs on code that has been automatically generated.

Safety-critical systems interact with the real world using sensors, actuators, and other devices. The software of these systems must be designed and verified very carefully. If not, such systems can be the cause of catastrophic consequences in terms of performance, safety, and security. While a significant amount of research has been done to improve the design of the software itself, there are, as of today, few methods for representing the software architecture and its interaction with the environment. And that's what AADL is all about.

This book is my modest contribution to show how AADL can be used when designing the architecture of software-critical systems. I wanted the book to be short and easy to understand, in the hopes that people can quickly learn the language and extend it for their own needs. The models, as well as the source code of our plug-ins, are available for free online in our GitHub repository,[90] and I hope developers will be inspired to create their own AADL models, extensions, and plug-ins. The AADL technology is now mature enough to be used, and it's time to help people leverage it for their own use.

---

[90]   https://github.com/juli1/aadl-book

Annexes

Bibliography

[AADL-BA]   AADL Behavior Annex Standard
              http://standards.sae.org/as5506/2/

[AADL-EMV2]   AADL Error Model Annex v2
              https://saemobilus.sae.org/content/as550
              6/1

[AADL-STD]   SAE AADL Standard
              http://standards.sae.org/as5506b/

[AADL-WS]   AADL general information website -
              http://www.aadl.info

[AGREE]   AGREE: Compositional Reasoning for AADL
              models
              http://www.mys5.org/Proceedings/2014/
              Day_1_S5_2014/2014-S5-Day1-
              13_Backes.pdf

[AGREE-MD]   Compositional verification of a medical
              device system
              http://dl.acm.org/citation.cfm?id=2527272

[ARP4761]   Guidelines and Methods for conducting the
              safety assessment process on civil airborne
              systems and equipment.
              https://saemobilus.sae.org/content/arp47
              61

[ASSERT]   J. Hugues, L. Pautet, P. Dissaux, M. Perrottin.
              "Using AADL to build critical real-time

ANNEXES

systems: Experiments in the IST-ASSERT project" http://taste.tuxfamily.org/wiki/images/b/b2/AADL_ASSERT_ERTS08.pdf

[COMPASS]   Correctness, Modeling and Performance of Aerospace Systems http://www.compass-toolset.org/

[D-MILS]   Distributed MILS http://www.d-mils.org

[EMF]   The Eclipse Modeling Framework http://www.eclipse.org/modeling/emf/. Also on Wikipedia https://en.wikipedia.org/wiki/Eclipse_Modeling_Framework

[LAST-LECT]   The Last Lecture - Randy Pausch http://www.cmu.edu/randyslecture/

[MARTE]   OMG MARTE http://www.omg.org/spec/MARTE/

[MASIW]   MASIW - Modular Avionics System Integrator Workplace https://forge.ispras.ru/projects/masiw-oss

[MED-DEV]   Larson, B. R., Zhang, Y., Barrett, S. C., Hatcliff, J., & Jones, P. L. (2015). Enabling Safe Interoperation by Medical Device Virtual Integration. *IEEE Design & Test*, *32*(5), 74-88.

[MIL-882D]   Department of Defense. Standard Practice for System Safety. http://www.system-safety.org/Documents/MIL-STD-882D.pdf

ANNEXES

[NIST02]   The Economic Impacts of Inadequate Infrastructure for Software Testing
https://www.nist.gov/sites/default/files/documents/director/planning/report02-3.pdf

[OMG-UML]   UML standard
http://www.omg.org/spec/UML/

[RESOLUTE]   Resolute: An Assurance case language for architecture models
http://dl.acm.org/citation.cfm?id=2663177

[SAVI]   System Architecture Virtual Integration
http://savi.avsi.aero/

[SAVI-ROI]   Summary Final Report for AFE58
http://savi.avsi.aero/wp-content/uploads/sites/2/2015/08/SAVI-AFE58-00-001_Summary_Final_Report.pdf

[SMACCM]   SMACCM: Secure Mathematically-Assured Composition of Control Models
http://loonwerks.com/projects/smaccm.html

[SYSML]   System Modeling Language
http://www.omgsysml.org/

[TASTE]   The Assert Set of Tools for Engineering
http://taste.tuxfamily.org

[UML]   Unified Modeling Language (UML)
http://uml.org/

ANNEXES

[WIKI-SA]   Wikipedia, Software Architecture
https://en.wikipedia.org/wiki/Software_ar
chitecture

[XTEXT]   Xtext website
http://www.eclipse.org/Xtext/

[XTEXT-BO]   Lorenzo Bettini. Implementing Domain-Specific Languages with Xtext and Xtend
https://www.packtpub.com/application-development/implementing-domain-specific-languages-xtext-and-xtend-second-edition

Tools

[AADL-INSP]   Ellidiss AADL Inspector
http://www.ellidiss.com/products/aadl-inspector/

[AADL-MOD]   Emacs and Vim modes for AADL
http://www.openaadl.org/aadl-mode.html

[MASIW Tool]   MASIW AADL tool environment
http://masiw.ispras.ru/

[OCARINA]   Command-line tools for AADL code generation
http://www.openaadl.org/ocarina.html

[OSATE]   Open Source AADL Tool Environment
http://osate.github.io/

[SCADE]   SCADE is a set of model-based tools for designing safety critical systems. SCADE is owned by ANSYS and was previously developed by Esterel-Technologies.

[SIMULINK]   Matlab Simulink
https://www.mathworks.com/products/si
mulink.html,
https://en.wikipedia.org/wiki/Simulink

Acronyms

AADL   Architecture Analysis and Design Language

ARP   Aerospace Recommended Practice

BA   Behavior Annex

CAN   Control Area Network

CEO   chief executive officer

CLI   command-line interface

CMU-SEI   Carnegie Mellon University Software
Engineering Institute

CSMA/CD   carrier-sense multiple access/collision
detection

CSV   comma separated values

CTO   chief technology officer

DARPA   Defense Advanced Research Projects
Agency

DSL   domain-specific language

EBSM   error behavior state machine

ANNEXES

EMF	Eclipse Modeling Framework
EMV2	Error Model Annex v2
ESA	European Space Agency
FHA	Functional Hazard Assessment
FMEA	Failure Mode and Effects Analysis
FTA	Fault Tree Analysis
GUI	graphical user interface
ICD	Interface Control Document
IDE	Interactive Development Environment
IP	Internet Protocol
ISPRAS	Institute for System Programming of the Russian Academy of Sciences
MBE	Model-Based Engineering
MPH	miles per hour
NIST	National Institute of Standards and Technology
OMG	Object Management Group
ROI	return on investment
SysML	System Modeling Language
TASTE	The Assert Set of Tools for Engineering
UI	User Interface
UML	Unified Modeling Language

VCS   Version-Control System

XMI   XML Metadata Interchange

Importing the Case Study into Our OSATE Workspace

Throughout this book, I use the same case study to demonstrate the different capabilities of AADL (and in another measure, OSATE). You need to import the AADL model into your OSATE workspace. The AADL project is available online, on a Git repository.[91] (If you aren't familiar with Git, it's a popular version-control system [VCS]). Eclipse includes an interface for checking out, checking in, and managing Git repositories. This section guides you through the steps to importing the AADL model.

---

[91]   https://en.wikipedia.org/wiki/Git

Step 1: Switch to the Git perspective.

Before doing anything, switch to the Git perspective in Eclipse so you can use all the Git-related functionalities. To do so, do the following, as shown in the figure below:

1. Click on the Window menu.
2. Select the Perspective option.
3. Select the Open Perspective option.
4. Select the Others option.

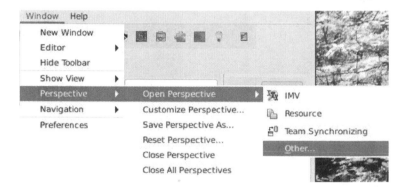

Menu options for opening a perspective

5. Then, select the Git perspective as follows:

Selecting the Git perspective

Step 2: Add the Git repository to your workspace.

Adding the Git repository to your environment will import the remote distributed repository on your computer. After doing this, you have a local copy of all the files on your local filesystem. To add this repository, follow these steps:

1. Select the icon to clone the Git repository.
2. Select the icon highlighted with a red border in the figure below (when you move your cursor over the icon, it should indicate this is used to clone a repository).

Icon to select to clone a Git repository

3. Then, enter these details about the repository, as shown in the figure below:
   - URI: https://github.com/juli1/aadl-book.git
   - host: github.com
   - repository path: /juli1/aadl-book.git

Parameters to specify when adding the aadl-book repository

Once the files are copied, the repository is added into the list of repositories in the Git perspective as shown below. Note that the path might be different for your system.

Git repository successfully added

Step 3: Import the AADL project into your workspace.

Finally, import the AADL project into your Eclipse environment using these steps:

1. Right-click the imported repository
2. Select the Import Projects option.

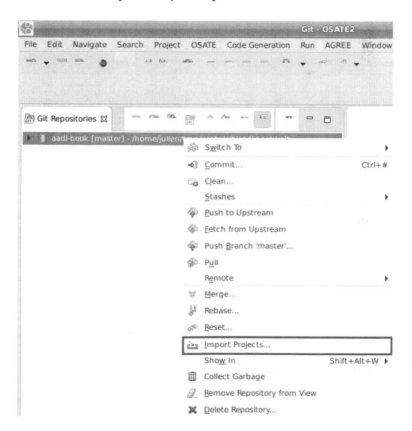

Contextual import menu

3. When a new window opens, click the Next button.

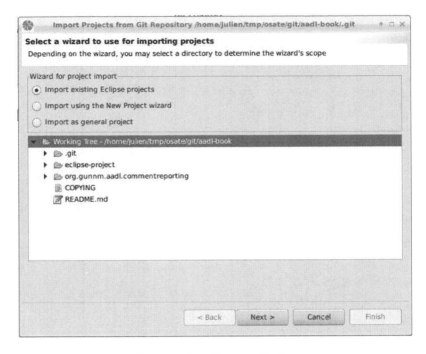

Importing the project

The next window asks for the name of the project to import. There are two projects:

- aadl-book: our AADL project of the case study
- org.gunnm.aadl.commentreporting: the source code of the project introduced in the Part 4 of this book.

4. Select the AADL project and click the Finish button.

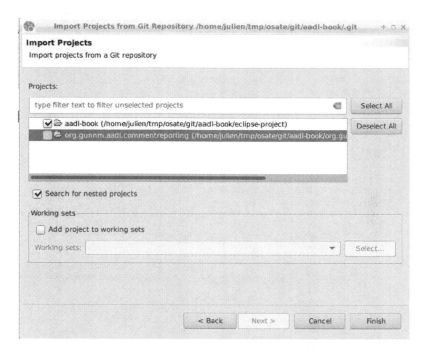

Importing the project – selecting the AADL project
(Note: directories vary according to your environment)

5. Switch back to the AADL perspective (use the same steps as for selecting the Git perspective but choose AADL instead of Git).
6. Open the directory and click on the files to open the textual AADL editor. You can now use and edit the AADL model of the case study.

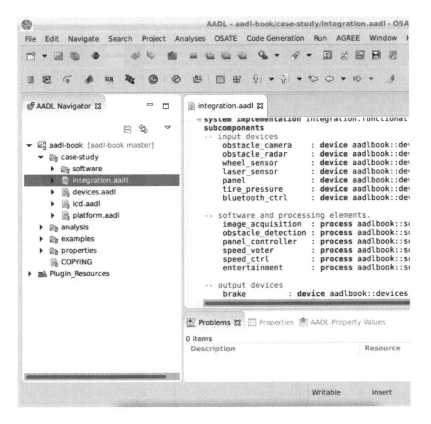

Model fully imported into OSATE

Getting Help

If you get stuck on a project and need more information, for example, how to model a particular system or develop a new analysis plug-in, you can consult the AADL community. It's well organized and has several mailing lists to help its members.[92] Some of the lists are dedicated to the standardization committee work, while others are designed for discussion with the user community.

Also, for more general help, there are groups dedicated to AADL and, more globally, Model-Based Engineering on social media sites such as LinkedIn. If you want to learn more about MBE, this can be a good place to start.

---

[92]   https://wiki.sei.cmu.edu/aadl/index.php/Mailing_List

Answers to Questions

Part 1 - Introduction

What are the main advantages of MBE?

MBE abstracts system concerns using models defined with a graphical and/or textual notation. Models are then used during the development process to communicate across teams, help certification efforts, or even create the final implementation. Adopting MBE avoids many of the mistakes that commonly occur with traditional development processes and ultimately reduces development costs.

What is AADL? UML? SysML?

AADL (Architecture Analysis and Design Language) is an architecture-modeling tool that uses a single, standardized textual and graphical notation and one single, consistent model. AADL is an SAE international standard with a common interchange format for reusing models across tools (the AADL textual notation).

UML (Unified Modeling Language) is a modeling language that captures various aspects of a system using a graphical notation. It uses multiple, potentially inconsistent models and is standardized by the Object Management Group (OMG).

SysML (System Modeling Language) is a modeling language dedicated to system engineering that captures system concerns using a graphical notation. Like UML, it uses multiple and potentially inconsistent models and is standardized by the OMG.

Where are most errors introduced in traditional development processes?

According to a study from NIST[93] [NIST02], about 70% of errors are introduced in the early design phases of traditional development processes. AADL captures and validates the system design earlier in the development process in order to get the system design right before implementation efforts begin. It fixes design issues in the design phases and avoids their propagation throughout later phases.

Where are most errors addressed in traditional development processes?

According to the same study from NIST[94] [NIST02], in traditional development processes, errors are addressed during testing and, more specifically, during integration testing. Discovering errors so late in the development process requires software to be updated multiples times and the coordination of efforts across different contractors. It also increases development costs and postpones product delivery. AADL captures integration concerns early in the

---

93

      https://www.nist.gov/sites/default/files/documents/director/planning/report02-3.pdf

94

      https://www.nist.gov/sites/default/files/documents/director/planning/report02-3.pdf

development process and avoids many of these potential errors.

Part 2 - What is AADL?

What are the component categories of AADL?

- hardware components: `processor, bus, memory,` and `device`
- software components: `process, thread, subprogram, thread group, subprogram group, data, virtual processor,` and `virtual bus`
- hybrid components: `system` and `abstract`

What is the difference between a component type and a component implementation?

The component type defines the outside of the component— how it communicates with the external world. The component type is made of a component category, its interfaces (ports and required/provided component access), and optionally, some properties.

The component implementation defines how the component provides/realizes a service internally, and the component's subcomponents and how they're organized. It contains subcomponents, defines their connection with the component interfaces, and, optionally, defines properties (or overrides the properties from the component type).

One component type can have multiple implementations. A component implementation refers to only one type.

ANSWERS TO QUESTIONS

How does AADL capture data transfer through software?

AADL captures data flows between software elements using ports. There are three categories of ports: `event port`, `data port`, and `event data port`. See Part 2 (What is AADL?) for more details about ports.

What is an AADL property?

An AADL property is a way to annotate the model with information that's helpful when using the model. It can define attributes of the system (e.g., weight of the system) or just augment its description (e.g., by adding comments).

Can you specify an AADL thread that outputs an event named wakeup every 10 seconds?

```
thread mythread
features
    wakeup : out event port;
properties
    dispatch_protocol => periodic;
    period => 10 sec;
end mythread;
```

Can you specify a simple software model with an AADL process bound to a processor and a memory?

```
system mysystem -- component type
```

```
end mysystem;

system implementation mysystem.i -- component
implementation
subcomponents
    p : process;
    cpu : processor;
    mem : memory;
properties
    actual_processor_binding => (reference
(cpu)) applies to p;
    actual_memory_binding => (reference (mem))
applies to p;
end mysystem.i;
```

Part 3 - System Analysis with AADL

Why do analysis tools use a system instance rather than a component declaration to perform an analysis?

The system instance contains all elements necessary to perform an analysis. The component declaration itself might be incomplete. For example, let's say you want to analyze all AADL threads that have the classifier mythread and check that the period is less than or equal to 10ms. So why not just process the AADL declaration? Because when using the component, the property can be refined.

Let's illustrate this with an example. First, we define the component and then a process that uses these thread components.

```
thread mythread
properties
    period => 10 ms;
end mythread;

process myprocess
end myprocess;

process implementation myprocess.i
subcomponents
    fast_thread : thread mythread;
    slow_thread : thread mythread;
properties
    period => 5 ms applies to fast_thread;
    period => 20 ms applies to slow_thread;
end myprocess.i;
```

If you analyze the mythread component, you can check that the period property is 10ms, so your requirements are met. However, in myprocess.i, the period properties are modified in the properties section so that the period value of slow_thread no longer meets the requirements.

The instance model contains the properties for **ALL** components: When instantiating the model, all properties values are resolved according to the overriding rules. Also, the instantiation process makes additional checks, such as verifying that all connections and flows are correct.

Which AADL architecture elements impact system latency?

The following components are used for the latency analysis: system, process, thread, device, and data.

The following properties are potentially used: `Latency`, `Period`, `Transmission_Time`, `Data_Size`, `Actual_Connection_Binding`, and `Actual_Processor_Binding`.

Why is an AADL annex necessary for fault modeling?

The core AADL language does not provide enough information to do a comprehensive fault modeling and safety analysis. Some elements are missing, such as the error behavior state machine (EBSM). One approach would have been to extend the core language with the content of EMV2, but that would have made the standard bigger and more difficult for newcomers to learn.

That's why an annex was used: It doesn't increase the size of the standard and complements the language for safety analysis. If you need to perform safety analysis, it's the way to go, but otherwise, you can just ignore it. That's one key objective of AADL: Make the language and tools modular to fit the needs of different users and development processes.

Can you identify the main difference between fault impact analysis and Fault Tree Analysis?

Fault impact analysis is a bottom-up approach: It analyzes the impact of each fault by looking at where it can propagate through the architecture. It starts at the initial fault (the cause) and finishes at the impacted component (the result).

Fault Tree Analysis is a top-down approach: It analyzes a failure and looks for all contributors to it. It starts at a fault (the result) and looks for any architectural elements that could have triggered it (the cause).

Part 4 - Extending AADL

What is OSATE? Eclipse? EMF? How do they relate to each other?

OSATE is an AADL modeling platform that supports both the textual and graphical notations of AADL. OSATE is built on top of the Eclipse platform.[95] In order to implement the modeling language, OSATE relies on the Eclipse Modeling Framework[96] (EMF), which provides the ability to implement modeling languages in Eclipse.

In which files of a plug-in project are Eclipse platform menus declared?

In an Eclipse project, new menus are added using the Eclipse extension mechanism. Extensions are declared in the `plugin.xml` file of the plug-in. On the other end, plug-in dependencies are declared in the `META-INF/MANIFEST.MF` file of the plug-in.

---

[95] http://www.eclipse.org/

[96] https://www.eclipse.org/modeling/emf/

How can you get all the subcomponent instances of a particular component instance?

To get all the component instances under a particular component instance, use the method getAllComponentInstances(). Then, to get the subcomponents under each component, use the getComponentInstances() method.

How can you get all the features of a particular component instance?

To get all the features of a component instance using the getFeatureInstances() method on the component. For example, for the componentInstance variable of type ComponentInstance, you would use the following call:

```
componentInstance.getFeatureInstances();
```

Can you write a method that takes a component instance in parameters and prints the component instance hierarchy on the standard output?

```
public static void printComponentHierarchyRec
      (ComponentInstance ci,
       int nSpaces, StringBuffer sb)
{
    for (int i = 0 ; i < nSpaces ; i++)
    {
        sb.append (" ");
```

```
    }
    sb.append (ci.getName());
    sb.append ("\n");
    for (ComponentInstance subco :
ci.getComponentInstances())
    {
        printComponentHierarchyRec(subco, nSpaces
+ 3, sb);
    }
}

public static void printComponentHierarchy
(ComponentInstance ci)
{
    StringBuffer sb = new StringBuffer ();
    printComponentHierarchyRec(ci, 0, sb);
    System.out.println(sb.toString());
}
```

Can you write a method that prints the name of all component instances for which the classifier name is "foobar"?

We assume the root system instance is in a variable called rootInstance.

```
rootInstance.getAllComponentInstances()
  .stream()
   .filter
    (c->c.getComponentClassifier().getName()
            .equalsIgnoreCase("foobar"))
              .forEach(c ->
           System.out.println (c.getName()));;
```

About the Author

Julien Delange currently lives in the United States of America and works as a senior software development engineer at Amazon Web Services in Seattle, Washington. He started to use computers very early: His first contact with a computer was with an Amstrad PC1512-MM his dad bought in the 1980s. Delange started programming when he was 12 years old and stayed addicted to programming and, more generally, all computer-science-related stuff.

He earned a master's degree and PhD in Paris, France (from *Université Pierre et Marie Curie* and *TELECOM ParisTech* engineering school) where he started to use AADL and contribute to the AADL standardization committee (mostly on AADL code generation). Delange wrote the POK separation kernel,[97] an ARINC653-compliant kernel that has been forked by ISPRAS under the name JetOS[98] and is now used in operational projects. From 2007 to 2010, he supervised the GISTR (*Genie Informatique des Systemes Temps-Réel*) master's degree at the EPITA engineering school in Paris, France. Delange worked at the European Space Agency from 2010 to 2012, where he continued to contribute to the AADL standard (designing the ARINC653 annex) and interact with the community. During that time, he was also a lead developer on the TASTE project[99] and applied the project to the aerospace and robotics fields. He joined the Carnegie Mellon University Software Engineering Institute in

---

[97] http://pok.tuxfamily.org/
[98] http://forge.ispras.ru/projects/chpok
[99] http://taste.tuxfamily.org/

ABOUT THE AUTHOR

2012 as a senior member of the technical staff where he worked on OSATE and safety and security analysis tools, and applied the AADL technology to other application domains, such as avionics, healthcare, and the military.

Made in the USA
San Bernardino, CA
08 January 2019